THE PLAN

THE PLAN

BIG IDEAS FOR AMERICA

RAHM EMANUEL
AND BRUCE REED

PUBLICAFFAIRS
New York

Published in the United States by PublicAffairs™,
a member of the Perseus Books Group.

Printed in the United States of America.

PublicAffairs books are available at special discounts
for bulk purchases in the U.S. by corporations,
institutions, and other organizations.
For more information, please contact the
Special Markets Department at the Perseus Books Group,
11 Cambridge Center,
Cambridge, MA 02142,
call (617) 252–5298,
or email special.markets@perseusbooks.com.

Book Design by Janet Tingey

Library of Congress Cataloging-in-Publication Data
is available from the Library
ISBN-13: 978-1-58648-412-5
ISBN-10: 1-58648-412-5

First Edition

10 9 8 7 6 5 4 3 2 1

CONTENTS

CONTENTS

To Amy, Zach, Ilana, and Leah
—R.E.

To Bonnie, Julia, and Nelson
—B.R.

PROLOGUE

LOST AND FOUND

"Who am I? Why am I here?" Insiders laughed when Ross Perot's running mate, Admiral James Stockdale, blurted out those words in the 1992 vice presidential debate. Yet in his own bumbling way, the late admiral had stumbled upon two of the most important and overlooked questions in American politics. As a newcomer making his prime-time debut, Stockdale can be forgiven for wondering who he was and why he was there. When we look around at the current political landscape, we wonder, what's Washington's excuse?

Most Americans think people in Washington have no idea what they're doing. From the budget deficit to Iraq to Hurricane Katrina, the Bush administration did a heck of a job calling government's competence into question.

But as two politicians who have spent most of the past two decades in Washington, we have encountered a more disturbing truth. Although Washington has its share of screw-ups and incompetents, most politicians here are pretty good at what they're doing. The trouble is, they're not always sure why they're doing it.

We're both dyed-in-the-wool, lifelong Democrats, but we can't help but notice that in recent years, both parties in Washington lost their way. Americans scratch their heads in wonder that Republicans and Democrats can't find common purpose. But the challenge is deeper: Each party needs to be clearer in its own purpose.

How could conservatism—which even with its many shortcomings was once a rigorous doctrine—have come to such a small-minded, unsatisfying demise? Republicans who rode to power on conservative ideals turned them into a hollow faith. Conservatism became a strategy for winning elections, not leading a nation—for staying in power, not respecting its limits. Conservative leaders forgot what made them conservatives in the first place: a recognition that rigid ideology has always been the God That Failed, and that no idea is good if it doesn't work.

Ironically, conservatives made government bigger, not smaller. In Senator John McCain's phrase, Washington Republicans spent like drunken sailors—a conservative administration leading the biggest domestic spending spree since Lyndon Johnson. No wonder Republicans are confused of late: They say their purpose is to get government off our backs, but they have little interest in or intention of doing so, and years of conclusive proof show that left to their own devices, they'll do just the opposite.

With Republicans confused and corrupted by being in

power, Democrats became so desperate to stop the damage that we often forgot to show where we'd like to lead the country instead. In the 1990s, Democrats began to define a new mission for the country and the party, with impressive results. But in recent years, our anger and frustration with the other side steered us away from our real strength: America hires Democrats to help solve problems, not to listen to us whine about them.

If all this were just about politics—one confused party somehow outmaneuvering the other—it might not matter that so many Republicans and some Democrats lost their way. But what's at stake is far more important than momentary partisan advantage. Today, America cannot afford to stumble. Our enemies are few, but after September 11, 2001, their intentions are clear. Our rivals also are few, but the rapid economic progress of competitors like India and China suggests that their aim is clear, too.

Lack of purpose comes at a heavy price. When the greatest superpower can't decide whether it even needs friends, the world is a more dangerous place. When the White House and Congress set out blindly to tax less and spend more, they literally mortgage the country's future to emerging economic rivals like China, which is all too happy to help us go deep in debt. When politicians in Washington care more about holding onto power than about what to do with it, they invite a culture of corruption that raids taxpayers' pockets and saps the nation's strength.

It shouldn't be this way. From the outset, America has been the most purposeful nation on earth. Americans work harder, plan more, and dream bigger than anyone else. One of the best-selling books so far this century is Rick Warren's *The Purpose Driven Life.* There is no excuse for American politics to be driven by anything less than purpose.

When historians look back on the early twenty-first century, they will have no trouble finding the precise moment when the Republican majority in Washington lost its way for good. On Palm Sunday weekend, 2005, then Majority Leader Tom DeLay—desperate to divert attention from his ethical troubles—called the House of Representatives into emergency session to try to rescue Terry Schiavo, a Florida woman who had spent fifteen years in a coma and showed no prospect of recovery. Senate Majority Leader Bill Frist, a capable doctor before he went into politics, watched a videotape of Schiavo and claimed to see miraculous signs of life. President Bush, on vacation from the rest of America's problems, rushed back from Crawford, Texas, to address the Schiavo crisis. Poor Terry Schiavo did not come back to life, even after the Republican Congress passed a law ordering federal courts to prolong her ordeal.

The Schiavo case was merely the most wrenching example of the pervasive pointlessness of current politics. The nation is at war, the government is broke, Washington is on the take—and yet the deeper the pile of problems, the shallower the political system's response. Faced with the long, arduous challenge of turning America around, Washington has instead become the patron saint of lost causes.

Washington isn't lost because those in charge are bad people. (Well, perhaps some of them are.) There's a larger reason: The old maps don't work anymore, and many of the old landmarks are gone.

Look how much the landscape has changed since 9/11. For all the terrors of the Cold War, we could count on a clear, identifiable enemy. All we had to do was outrun the Soviet bear. Today, we're at war with a radical totalitarianism we cannot comprehend, which has its roots in a culture with which we are scarcely familiar. We knew what it meant to win the Cold War: contain Soviet expansion, expand freedom and democracy, and maintain our military edge. Five years into the war on terror, we still don't know how victory will be defined, and Americans are not at all certain that we're winning.

The economic compact we grew up with is largely gone, too. Not so long ago, Americans could count on spending an entire career working for the same company. People knew of at least one sure ticket: If they worked hard enough, they were bound to get ahead. Even people without fancy educations could find a good job. And that good job brought its own certainties: health care, a pension, and sometimes a promotion. When the country grew, so did wages. Although the American economy is still fundamentally strong, Americans can no longer count on any of those assurances. A good job is hard to find, no job is secure, and paychecks aren't growing. The greatest source of anxiety is that all that hard work doesn't pay off.

Finally, the social fabric that used to knit us together is hanging by a thread. The American family has been through decades of turmoil. Forced to work more, parents spend less time with their children and more time worrying about them. We are endlessly torn between community and convenience: a famously gregarious nation of people at risk of turning into iPods passing in the night.

Security, opportunity, and community are the foundations on which American society was built. In the blink of an eye, they've been washed out from under us. We sense the peril, but cannot find our footing. Our leaders are suspended in animation, like cartoon characters who have run off the cliff—afraid to look down for fear that they will fall to the ground below.

So instead of facing the need to build new foundations, American politics struggles mightily to cover up for the loss of everything we used to take for granted. The 2004 presidential election pitted one party's sense of loss against the other's. Republicans tried to make their sputtering strategy for the war on terror sound as reassuring as

America's strategy for winning the Cold War. In President Bush's words, "You're either with us or against us." For millions of overworked, underpaid families concerned about the culture, Republicans had another simple, if unrelated, answer: a ban on same-sex marriage. Democrats, meanwhile, responded to legitimate fears about the vanishing economic compact between employees and employers by making believe that it would magically reappear if we complained loudly enough about outsourcing. In a split decision, Republicans won the 2004 contest, two existential anxieties to one.

Americans are frustrated and perplexed by politics becoming even meaner, more polarized, and less purposeful in the wake of 9/11 than it was before. President Bush said he faced the same challenges at home and abroad as Franklin Roosevelt. The comparison is revealing, but not in the way Bush intended. FDR inherited a country divided by the Depression as it faced war, and united it; Bush on 9/11 inherited a country that longed to be united, and further divided it. FDR inherited a depression and gave America the greatest middle-class expansion it has ever known. Bush inherited the longest economic boom in history and gave the middle class the highest anxiety in memory.

A deeper challenge remains, even as Bush fades from view. It's no accident that our political breakdown coincides with the collapse of the old economic, cultural, and security arrangements. The ugly political polarization of the past decade is the shrapnel from another clash of civilizations—the old certainties we can't quite hold onto colliding with the new certainties we're fumbling in the dark to find.

The trouble with politics today is that it is more consumed with solving political problems than with solving the country's problems. Since 9/11, Republicans have sought mightily to turn national security into a political project. When our country was attacked, partisan politics was the last thing on most Americans' minds. Indeed, an end to partisan bickering would have been the one welcome casualty in the war on terror. The Bush White House chose instead to put politics first, exploiting Americans' fears in order to make partisan gains in the 2002 midterm elections and hold onto the White House in 2004. The Republican playbook for the post–9/11 world has been to make Americans fear Democrats and terrorists as twin threats to the nation's security.

Yet, in their own way, some Democrats bought into Karl Rove's logic that the most important challenge of our time is how to win an election. If Republicans could get away with divisive, smashmouth, take-no-prisoners politics, frustrated Democrats wondered, why couldn't we? Much as Democrats lamented Bush's policy failures, we spent much of his time in office envying his electoral success. We cursed Rove for wrecking the country, then longed for handlers who could keep up with his playbook. On both sides of the aisle, the political debate sunk to a new low: Ask not what your country can do for you, ask focus groups what they want you to do for them.

If not for the consequences, the bipartisan identity crisis might have been entertaining. Republicans found themselves trapped in the limbo of Bush's "compassionate conservatism," unsure at any given moment whether government should expand or contract. They couldn't run fast enough from Bush's record, but they had no national agenda to run on in its place. Democrats became the party of second opinions, wandering from one pathologist to the next. Consultants told Democrats to talk more about God; bloggers told them to talk trash about Bush; political self-help books urged them to use their words, rediscover their values, and stand and fight for what they used to believe in.

We've spent much of our careers helping Democrats win. But in our view, that is the right answer to the wrong question. The politics of the Bush era, on both sides of the aisle, was based on a mistaken premise. America is not a partisan prize or political project. Without a map to the challenges of the new era, all political roads lead to ruin.

This book is based on the premise that instead of mourning old arrangements, we should make new ones. Seventy-five years ago, at a time of similar uncertainty, FDR told the Commonwealth Club:

> New conditions impose new requirements upon Government and those who conduct Government. . . . Faith in America, faith in our tradition of personal responsibility, faith in our institutions, faith in ourselves demands that we recognize the new terms of the old social contract. . . . Failure is not an American habit, and in the strength of great hope we must all shoulder our common load.

This book is a first draft of the new conditions, new requirements, and new terms that our new era will demand. Part 1 explains where the old political battles and arrangements have failed the nation—and how we can get beyond them. Part 2 lays out The Plan—a new social contract for the twenty-first century and a new patriotism and responsibility to make it happen. No matter your political leanings—Democrat, Republican, Independent, or none of the above—we hope the ideas in these pages will inspire you to think about the great challenges ahead. Whether or not you agree with the specifics of our plan, we urge you to hold us all to the spirit behind it: There is nothing wrong with America—or either party—that can't be set right by finding the courage, the ideas, and the energy to solve our country's problems.

PART ONE

WHAT WENT WRONG

CHAPTER 1

HACKS AND WONKS

Before America can carry out the policies in The Plan, we need to recognize where politics has led us astray.

Strip away the job titles and party labels, and you will find two tribes of people in Washington: political Hacks and policy Wonks. Hacks come to Washington because anywhere else they'd be bored to death. Wonks come here because nowhere else could they bore so many to death. These divisions extend far beyond the Hack havens of political campaigns and consulting firms and the Wonk ghettos of think tanks on Dupont Circle. Some journalists are Wonks, but most are Hacks. Some columnists are Hacks, but most are Wonks. All members of Congress pass themselves off as Wonks, but many got elected as Hacks. Lobbyists are Hacks who make money pretending to be Wonks. The *Washington Monthly,* the *New Republic,* and the political blogosphere consist largely of Wonks pretending to be Hacks.

After two decades in Washington, we have come to the

conclusion that the gap between Republicans and Democrats is as nothing compared to the one between these two tribes. Wonks think all Hacks are creatures from another planet, like James Carville. Hacks share Paul Begala's view that Wonks are all "propeller heads." Wonks think they're smarter than Hacks. Hacks think that if being smart makes someone a Wonk, they'd rather be stupid.

We should know. When we began working together in the Clinton White House, we came from different tribes—one of us a Hack, the other a Wonk. (We're not telling which.) We made a deal to teach each other the secrets, quirks, and idioms of our respective sects. Together, we took on a series of issues—crime, welfare, family values—that had been stuck at the crossroads between politics and policy for a generation.

Along the way, we discovered uncomfortable truths about both our circles. Wonks could be the most naive smart people in the world, overflowing with knowledge about what could work in theory, clueless as to what would work in practice. Don't doubt Albert Einstein's intelligence because he thought that "the hardest thing in the world to understand is the income tax"; blame the Wonk genius at the IRS who designed the form. When all you have is policy, the whole world is a programmatic solution. After too many encounters with the Clinton administration's Wonks, Senator Daniel Patrick Moynihan once warned us, "Anyone who admits that he doesn't have all the answers will always be welcome in my office."

In 1993, a series of high-profile murders produced a groundswell of public support for the Clinton crime bill, which would later put 100,000 new community police officers on the street, ban assault weapons, and stiffen penalties for violent crime. One multiagency group of Wonks, terrified that the public might get what it wanted, formed a violence prevention task force whose sole purpose seemed to be churning out ideas the public would not support. The task force included one of the most ridiculously named subcommittees of all time, the Subgroup on Place. Hacks still laugh about it.

On the other hand, if Wonks could be comically off base, Hacks were often downright dangerous. In 1993, some of the president's top communications strategists tried to postpone a bill-signing ceremony for a few weeks to arrange a better photo opportunity. A Wonk had to point out that under the Constitution, if the president fails to sign a bill within ten days while the Congress is adjourned, the bill is pocket-vetoed and does not become law. Wonks still laugh about that, too.

In 1995, President Clinton brought in Dick Morris, a smart but troubled Republican operative, to get the White House's politics back on track. Morris turned out to be a useful spur to the bureaucracy, because at the White House we deployed our own Madman Theory: If the agencies wouldn't go along with our sensible proposals, we told them that the president might just listen to Dick Morris's nuttiest suggestions. Agency productivity soared as a result.

Just as the Wonks had a program for every problem, Morris had a poll number for every program. It became our job to shoot down Morris's Hack ideas if they didn't pass Wonk muster. Every week, Morris had at least one notion crazy enough to get us laughed out of office if we had tried to enact it. One time he proposed putting voluntary warning labels on violent toys, so that parents would know, for example, that a toy gun was actually a toy gun.

Throughout history, Hacks and Wonks have been the yin and yang of politics. And in every administration, Wonks and Hacks fight it out. The measure of a great president is his ability to make sense of them both. A president must know the real problems on Americans' minds. For that he needs Hacks. But ultimately, he needs policies that will actually solve those problems. For that he needs Wonks.

Putting Politics First

But in the last few years, something terrible has destroyed our political equilibrium. The political world suffered a devastating outbreak of what might be called Rove Flu—a virus that destroys any part of the brain not dedicated to partisan political manipulation. Now Hacks are everywhere. Like woolly mammoths on the run from Neanderthals, Wonks are all but extinct.

Although Hacks have never been in short supply in our nation's capital, the rise of one-party rule in Washington over the past four years unleashed an all-out Hack attack. Every issue, every debate, every job opening was seen as an opportunity to gain partisan advantage. Internal disagreement was stifled, independent thought discouraged, party discipline strictly enforced—and that's just how they treated their friends.

President Bush husbanded some big policy changes through the Republican Congress. Unfortunately, his policies were better at causing problems than solving them. Tax cuts fueled huge deficits. The Medicare prescription drug law, at a ten year cost of nearly a trillion dollars, did more to raise seniors' blood pressure than to treat it.

Democrats are understandably eager to blame all these epic failures on ideology. To be sure, Bush ran perhaps the most partisan and ideological White House in the modern era. His party's long-standing fondness for tax cuts evolved into a pathological need to ask less of the wealthy. His unilateralism left America with fewer allies and a greater share of the burden and the bills. But ideology was just one reason the president's agenda failed. The deeper reason was darker and more disturbing: The Bush White House was so obsessed with how to profit politically from its agenda that it never even asked whether its policies would actually work. It should come as no surprise that they didn't.

Journalist Ron Suskind first sounded this warning in January 2003, in an extraordinary *Esquire* interview with John DiIulio, the brilliant academic who had resigned from Bush's faith-based initiative the previous year. DiIulio told Suskind, "There is no precedent in any modern White House for what is going on in this one: a complete lack of a policy apparatus. What you've got is everything—and I mean everything—being run by the political arm." As if to prove the point, the White House got DiIulio to disavow the allegations as soon as they became public.

Every White House worries too much about politics. The Bush White House worried about little else. As DiIulio put it:

> The lack of even basic policy knowledge, and the only casual interest in knowing more, was somewhat breathtaking: discussions by fairly senior people who meant Medicaid but were talking Medicare; near instant shifts from discussing any actual policy pros and cons to discussing political communications, media strategy, etc.

By the time Treasury Secretary Paul O'Neill left the Bush administration, he actually pined for the less political days of his time in the Nixon White House. As O'Neill told Suskind for *The Price of Loyalty,* the book about his time working for Bush, "The biggest difference between then and now is that our group was mostly about evidence and analysis, and Karl, Dick, Karen, and the gang seemed to be mostly about politics."

Any president who lets people like Karl Rove make the key decisions is sure to get the big ones wrong. Even the most gifted Hacks, like Rove and Morris, have an insurmountable blind spot: The only results they understand come from polling.

Perhaps the best recent example of paint-by-numbers politics was the Medicare prescription drug bill. The bill was conceived of as a way to win over elderly voters who were fed up with high drug prices. But in order to placate pharmaceutical interests, the bill was written to prohibit the government from negotiating lower drug prices. To appease conservatives angry over the bill's price tag, it was made deliberately confusing. It pays 75 percent of the first $2,250 (after a $250 deductible), then nothing until a recipient's out-of-pocket costs have reached $3,600. The collective result: Soon everyone came to hate it—seniors, conservatives, pharmacists, and even the Republican members of Congress who voted for it.

One prominent Hack, Tom Scully—then an assistant secretary in the Department of Health and Human Services, later a health care lobbyist—allegedly threatened to fire Richard Foster, a career government actuary, if he revealed how much the prescription drug bill would explode Medicare spending. Remember the good old days when Republicans went to jail for covering up burglaries and conducting covert wars against communism? Now they're under fire for covering up massive social spending. No wonder conservatives are unhappy. It's as if Oliver North were running a secret Head Start program in the White House basement.

The Compassion of the Conservative

President Bush served as Hack-in-Chief even when he studiously pretended not to be doing so. Consider his loftiest attempts to describe his governing philosophy: compassionate conservatism, changing the tone in Washington, the Responsibility Era, and the Ownership Society.

From an electoral standpoint, each of these phrases was a brilliant political slogan. In the 2000 campaign, Bush's pitch for compassionate conservatism put a kinder, gentler face on a Republican Party still reeling from the 1995 budget battle when Republicans shut down the government in an attempt to force deep cuts in Medicaid, Medicare, education, and the environment. Bill Clinton, no slouch at campaigning, called it the cleverest slogan he'd ever heard. Unfortunately, it also proved to be one of the emptiest.

Compassionate conservatism was never primarily a policy agenda. First and foremost, it was a political project. Just as Peggy Noonan had coined "a kinder, gentler nation" to inoculate Bush's father against the dark side of Reaganism, Karl Rove and company used "compassionate conservatism" to imply that George W. Bush wouldn't be another antigovernment Republican. As a short-term political gambit, it worked famously. As a governing philosophy, however, it was a disaster—too much faith, not enough works. Bush's compassion agenda died by his own hand in May 2001, when he called for a new war on poverty the same week he threatened the Senate he would veto anything less than his full $1.6-trillion tax cut. Bush proved that Bill Clinton had been right back in 1999, when he said:

> This compassionate conservatism has a great ring to it, you know. It sounds soooo good. And near as I can tell, here's what it means: It means, "I like you. I do. And I would like to be for the patients' bill of rights, and I'd like to be for closing the gun show loophole, and I'd like not to squander the surplus and, you know, save Social Security and Medicare for the next generation. I'd like to raise the minimum wage. I'd like to do these things. But I just can't. And I feel terrible about it."

Bush's promise to change the tone in Washington met the same fate. Politically, the phrase was bold and breathtaking. The country longed to move beyond the brutish hyperpartisanship of the late 1990s; here was a Republican candidate promising to rein in his party's worst attack-dog instincts. As president, however, Bush did what had seemed impossible: His administration actually managed to make Washington more partisan and the tone of political debate more vicious and superficial. Bush came into office promising to be a compassionate conservative, soon left us yearning for a competent conservative, and seems destined to be remembered for presiding over the heyday of the corrupt conservative.

But the Waterloo for Bush's political generals and their armies of Hacks turned out to be his sweeping ambitions to "usher in a Responsibility Era" and create an "Ownership Society." Clinton's greatest achievements, from reforming welfare in 1996 to bringing the budget into surplus in 1998, had shown that more than any other value, *responsibility* had the power to solve seemingly intractable problems. But even that proved too much for the Bush administration to deliver. After record budget deficits, repeated political scandals, rampant bureaucratic incompetence, and the president's stubborn refusal to admit mistakes, hold anyone accountable, or level with the American people, it became clear that the Responsibility Era would not begin until Bush left office.

The central promise of Bush's 2004 reelection campaign—an Ownership Society—sounded every bit as good. Alas, the White House was no more serious about addressing the nation's long-term fiscal problems than its immediate ones. As Rove openly explained to any who would listen, the real beauty of the Ownership Society was not substantive, but political. GOP strategists believed that in one fell swoop, Bush could replace FDR's New Deal with a lasting Republican legacy. "With $5,000 in stock, you become 18% more Republican," Grover Norquist of Americans for Tax Reform told *Business Week*.

Encouragingly, Bush and Rove paid a heavy political

price for their policy hubris. Bush's Social Security proposal, shaped by Hacks for a political campaign, couldn't survive even the lightest Wonk scrutiny. It would have forced the government to borrow trillions of dollars, put individuals' nest eggs at greater risk, and done nothing to keep Social Security from running short of revenue in thirty years. It promised individuals ownership by advancing them money to put in private accounts, but would have required them to reimburse the Social Security system for the money it lent them—plus interest—and left them with no recourse if their investments went bad. It didn't fly.

Hacks Gone Wild

Republicans have learned the hard way that the American people are a lot smarter than either the Hacks or the Wonks imagine. For all the talk in both parties about the urgent need to win one constituency or another, most Americans apply the same political yardstick: They vote for what works. There aren't enough Hacks, even in Washington, to sell policies that don't work—although that never stopped Bush from trying.

Yet as Americans survey the damage from six years of Hacks Gone Wild, bad policy is only the beginning. In his Farewell Address, another Republican president, Dwight Eisenhower, warned of an "iron triangle" of legislators, bureaucrats, and private contractors eager to increase arms production. Today's Republicans have created a kind of Hack triangle from the White House to Congress to K Street lobbyists. Tom DeLay may be gone, but those in office will still do anything to stay there; those who make their living off those in office stop at nothing to keep them there. And with so many private interests at stake, the country's problems have had to wait in line.

In the old days, a popular American business model was planned obsolescence: making products that wouldn't last long so that consumers had to buy a replacement. The Republican political model is planned incompetence: When bureaucrats screw up or government programs don't work, that only reinforces public skepticism about government.

We can survive a can't-do administration; we've done it before. But the United States cannot survive the loss of its can-do spirit. Unfortunately, the current administration has been a failure of competence *and* ideology. Instead of honest conservatism, we've been stuck with the opposite: more government and less effectiveness. The rugged individualism of "those who can, do" has given us "those who can't, govern."

Hack government could get by in the old era, when one party's Hacks simply had to outwit the other's. Now, the challenges government faces are too hard to fake it, and the consequences of failure too dire.

We knew Hack fever had gotten out of hand when the producers of *Fear Factor* proposed a reality show called *Red/Blue,* modeled on *American Idol,* to find the next Karl

Rove. But we've known enough Hacks to realize how little the nation stands to gain from churning out more of them.

In order to turn the country around, Democrats have to learn that lesson, too.

CHAPTER 2

THE FRAME GAME

The Republican political model may have run the country into the ground, but it did succeed in its central objective: flummoxing Democrats. With Bush leaving a trail of unsolved problems, Democrats should have been in Wonk heaven fixing them. But every time Republicans won an election with divisive partisan gamesmanship, the Democratic response was "Why can't *our* Hacks do that?"

When we first came to Washington twenty years ago, the Democrats' cause seemed truly hopeless. Midway through the presidency of Ronald Reagan, Congresswoman Pat Schroeder said, "There are three things Democrats must do to take back the White House. Unfortunately, no one knows what they are." Even in the heartbreaking defeats of 2000 and 2004, Democrats did better at the polls than twenty years ago. Of late, we've been losing presidential elections in overtime or by a late field goal, not at the opening whistle.

But the core of our problem in 2004 was familiar: From

Franklin Roosevelt to Bill Clinton, the Democratic Party made its name by building a better life for the middle class. We can't win elections when the middle class doesn't vote for us.

It was no surprise for Democrats to lose white men and evangelicals, who have voted overwhelmingly Republican for decades. But in the 2004 election, we also lost white women, married people, couples with children, high school graduates, college graduates, people over thirty, and voters with incomes above $30,000. Our unlikely coalition consisted of two groups with little in common—high school dropouts and those with a postgraduate education.

As political analyst Charlie Cook has pointed out, one of the best recent measures of voting behavior is whether you live closer to a Wal-Mart (which sells guns), meaning you'll vote Republican, or a Starbucks (which sells lattes), indicating you're a Democrat. Some joke that the trick is appealing to the all-important swing voters—tens of millions of overcaffeinated gun owners who live close to both. Meanwhile, the forgotten middle class is in line at Dunkin' Donuts.

Word Search

If the Democratic Party's electoral challenge is straightforward—to show ordinary people that we can help them get ahead—the debate many Democrats have been having with themselves is as far removed from that challenge as it could get. Republicans have been trapped in more or less the same political rut for the past thirty years: Since they don't really believe in a positive agenda, they win elections by raising doubts about us. Democrats' rebuttal should be obvious enough: Unlike Republicans, we have ways to solve the country's problems, and sharing those ideas should put all doubts to rest. But too often in recent years, Democrats ignored that persuasive, winning strategy and tried to beat Republicans at their own game instead.

In the 2004 national election, an innocent voter could be forgiven for concluding that the Democrats' unifying principle was not how much we wanted to transform the country but how much we wanted to beat the other side. All we seemed to care about was winning—and consequently, we weren't very good at that, either. We didn't take a chance on our own ideas, for fear of losing. Instead of truly looking for answers to the country's problems, we hired consultants to look for slogans.

Losing wasn't the only price Democrats paid for that election: We passed up an opportunity to define ourselves to the nation, too. Like Al Gore in 2000, John Kerry had good ideas, but campaigned primarily on what was wrong with his opponent. The last Democratic presidential nominee to put his agenda at the center of his campaign was Clinton in 1996. (Not to belabor the point, but Clinton won.) That means it has been ten years since the Democratic Party effectively told the American people what we stand for.

If you asked political professionals in our party what is the matter with Democrats, many would say that we're not "getting our message out." Certainly, conservatives have developed a more effective echo chamber, and there's no doubt that presidential elections are won by the candidate best able to convey his campaign message.

But any party that writes off its defeats as a communications problem is doomed to repeat them. The American people are *much* smarter and more sophisticated than politicians and political professionals give them credit for. Nine times out of ten, what Hacks euphemistically call "a communications problem" has little to do with how well a campaign communicated and everything to do with what it was trying to say. In the wake of the 2004 election, it should not have taken long for Democrats to realize that you can't win an argument unless you make one. Instead, the party's troubles spawned an entire industry of self-help books, speeches, and seminars designed to reassure Democrats that all the old party needs is a new coat of paint.

The leading proponent of this reassurance is Professor George Lakoff, a University of California linguist and author of the best-selling tract *Don't Think of an Elephant!* Lakoff's book, a compilation of speeches on what he calls "Frame Semantics," has sold about a quarter million copies since 2004.

Why have so many Democrats snapped up Lakoff's manual? Because it tells them exactly what they want to hear.

As might be expected from a linguistics professor and self-proclaimed "metaphor analyst," the book contends that Democrats' biggest problem is the words we use. All progressives need to do to win the political debate, he argues, is to change the conceptual "frame" in which it takes place. According to Lakoff, Democratic arguments are bouncing off the electorate's collective subconscious because conservatives have set the frame and we haven't.

To be fair, Lakoff isn't wrong about everything. He understands the importance of values and an agenda. He calls the lack of ideas "hypocognition"—which he says was first discovered in a Tahitian tribe where suicide was rampant because it lacked the concept of grief. One man's frame is another man's pine box.

But Lakoff is flat-out wrong to suggest that Democrats are losing just because Republicans know all the right words. His favorite example is that conservatives learned to call tax cuts "tax *relief*." He's right that Republicans make a fetish out of using the most misleading, Orwellian words they can find. But let's be honest: Bush didn't manage to pass his tax cuts because he called them "tax relief." (Most of the time, he called them "tax cuts.") Bush got the chance to pass his disastrous tax cuts because Democrats were too slow to offer real tax reform proposals of our own. The tax debate illustrates what Al From, who founded the Democratic Leadership Council, has astutely observed: In a country with three self-identified conservatives for every two self-identified liberals, when neither side's agenda is sufficiently compelling, Republicans usually win by default.

The real danger of Lakoff's analysis is that it reinforces Democrats' favorite excuse—that Republicans have succeeded by pulling the wool over Americans' eyes, and that we'll start winning as soon as we learn the same dark arts. Here's how he explains Bill Clinton's success:

> He stole the other side's language. He talked about "welfare reform," for example. He said, "The age of big government is over." He did what he wanted to do, only he took their language and used their words to describe it. It made them very mad. Very smart technique.

Clinton did, indeed, reclaim issues that Republicans had trotted out in campaigns but never acted on in office. But deeds carried the day for him, not words. Clinton ended welfare as we know it and the era of big government on his own terms, not the Republicans'.

Some Democrats want to believe that we can stand in front of the mirror and practice the words to win America back. "Ever wonder how the radical right has been able to convince average Americans to repeatedly vote against their own interests?" Ariana Huffington says in plugging Lakoff's book, "It's the framing, stupid!" One glowing reviewer declared, "While Democrats were campaigning as if policy mattered, Republicans were waging their campaign on a far more fundamental, and more powerful, psychological level."

Lakoff insists that when arguing against the other side, the main principle of framing is "Do not use their language. Their language picks out a frame—and it won't be the frame you want." What he doesn't realize, however, is that the whole notion that words matter more than reason *is* the Republicans' frame, and it's the wrong one for the country's future.

If we believed in conspiracy theories, we'd think that only Karl Rove could dream up the idea of a linguistics professor from Berkeley urging Democrats to "practice reframing every day, on every issue." Lakoff even sounds like Rove when he says (approvingly!) that Republicans offer the "strict father" worldview and Democrats the "nurturant parent." He describes 9/11 in phallic terms: "Towers are symbols of phallic power, and their collapse reinforces the idea of loss of power. Another kind of phallic imagery was more central here: the planes penetrating the towers with a plume of heat, and the Pentagon, a vaginal image from the air, penetrated by the plane as missile." With frames like that, who needs enemies?

The Matter with Kansas

Highbrows like Lakoff and street fighters like Rove share the same Hack fallacy that we can game history to our advantage. In truth, we don't get to pick and choose between the great challenges the country faces. Even in calmer times, voters decided what was on their minds, not politicians. Today, we have no choice but to play the hand we're dealt: a long war against terrorism, a long struggle to compete economically, and a long way to go to build a culture of community here at home.

Republicans spent the past six years trying to stack the political deck in their favor by downplaying the country's long-term concerns and playing up the few remaining issues where they could claim any momentary public trust. In the 2002 campaign, Republicans ignored the economy, which was struggling, and cynically exploited the post–9/11 concern about security. In the 2004 campaign, the White House couldn't be sure from week to week which of their policies—economic or security—would be the bigger failure, so they hedged their bets with constitutional amendments on same-sex marriage. In early 2006, with voters clamoring for change in Washington, Rove gave a speech explaining the Republican strategy of once again using the midterm elections to question Democratic credentials on security.

Democrats followed the Rove playbook in reverse. In 2002, we tried to change the subject from security to the economy, and let Bush beat us with a silly debate over the Department of Homeland Security—which had originally been Democrats' idea, and a flawed one at that. In 2004, the Kerry campaign tried to avoid values issues like same-sex marriage, went back and forth between the economy and security, and ran hot and cold on Iraq. Republicans were in a stronger position to carry out their game plan, since they had the larger megaphone of the White House, but both sides had the same strategy: Ignore your own shortcomings and exploit the other side's.

No one should be surprised by the Republicans' tactical cynicism—we can't say they didn't warn us. Their political model isn't built to run the country; it's just designed to outrun the opposing party. What's more surprising is Democrats' willingness to play along. If George Lakoff's best seller *Don't Think of an Elephant!* urges Democrats to change the frame of the political debate, Thomas Frank's best seller *What's the Matter with Kansas?* implores Democrats to join Republicans in trying to change the subject.

Frank's book, an entertaining hatchet job on his home state of Kansas, attempts to tell the story of why many working- and middle-class Americans left the Democratic Party over the past thirty years. Kansas turns out not to be a very useful example, because the state hasn't elected a Democrat to the Senate since 1932. But Frank explores the state and his own upper-middle-class suburb in an effort to discover why so many voters put cultural issues ahead of economic ones. In a chapter called "What's the Matter with America?" he declares, "People getting their fundamental interests wrong is what American political life is all about. This species of derangement is the bedrock of our civic order."

In Frank's view, ordinary Americans have been duped into caring about the wrong issues, like guns, abortion, and security, when they ought to be voting their pocketbooks. He blames conservatives for fueling this cultural backlash—and heaps special blame on Democrats for abandoning class warfare:

> Democrats no longer speak to the people on the losing end of a free-market system that is becoming more brutal and more arrogant by the day. By dropping the class language that once distinguished them sharply from Republicans they have left themselves vulnerable to cultural wedge issues like guns and abortion and the rest whose hallucinatory appeal would ordinarily be far overshadowed by material concerns.

If working-class Americans feel like victims of an elitist conspiracy, Frank seems to say, it's Democrats' fault for not making them feel like victims of a capitalist one.

Frank is right to question Republican motives, but wrong to question Americans'. Voting on cultural issues instead of economic ones doesn't make people deranged dupes. If it's all right for affluent suburbanites to choose candidates based on abortion rights or the environment, it's insulting to suggest that blue-collar workers are wrong to make faith or conscience, not money, their bottom line.

Democrats won't win back those voters by changing the subject or raising the volume. The best way to trump the

Republicans' gambit is to stop trying to play their game. Instead of looking for ways to turn every issue to partisan advantage, we should start tackling big problems to the country's advantage. As the Bush administration's collapse demonstrated, it's not possible to change the subject for long. Democrats can't ignore security; Republicans can't ignore the economy; and both sides will have to learn to solve class and cultural concerns, not just stoke them.

Giving an Answer

The final myth that Democrats must leave behind is the idea that "oppose, oppose, oppose" is a successful formula for an opposition party to escape being in the opposition. A successful opposition must oppose and propose, and do both well. Democrats in Congress have an obligation to stand firm against the Republicans whenever they're wrong, which is all too often. At the same time, however, we have an obligation to ourselves and to the future to suggest a clear alternative path for the country to follow. As Mark Penn found in a recent survey for *Blueprint* magazine, three out of four Americans—and five out of six rank-and-file Democrats—are more interested in hearing Democrats' agenda than what's wrong with Republicans'.

In the end, the purpose of politics isn't to say the right words or strike the right notes, it's to find the right answer. That takes courage, not calculation. Ten years ago, Bill Clinton faced perhaps the most difficult decision of his presidency—whether to sign a sweeping welfare reform bill into law. Even those of us who had worked with him for years didn't know what he would decide. The bill posed an excruciating dilemma. On the one hand, it made good on his signature promise to "end welfare as we know it": requiring recipients to work, providing child care and health care so they could work, cracking down on absent parents who owed child support, and helping people find jobs and independence so they wouldn't need the welfare system anymore. By vetoing two earlier bills, Clinton had preserved the guarantee of health care and nutrition for poor children, and had forced the Republican Congress to provide more money to put people to work. He knew from history that if he vetoed this bill, the chance to reform a broken system might never come his way again. On the other hand, Republicans had insisted on mean-spirited cuts in benefits for legal immigrants, which made Clinton's blood boil. Moreover, many Democrats had never shared his desire to fundamentally reform welfare in the first place. Democrats in Congress were evenly divided, for and against the bill. Within the administration, those of us who supported it were badly outnumbered.

The outside world saw the whole debate as a political decision—but for Clinton, politics was the least of the concerns. He was well on his way to reelection, and had done more than enough through executive action to satisfy the electorate—issuing executive orders to increase child support collections, impose time limits and work requirements, and require teenaged welfare mothers to live at home and stay in school as a condition of public assistance. He had approved welfare reform experiments for forty-three states, more than all previous administrations combined. If Clinton had wanted to decide the issue on the politics, he could simply have vetoed the bill to keep his party happy or could have signed it to neutralize the issue. But as a governor, Clinton had spent more time in welfare offices than any politician in Washington. He wanted to do right by people like Lillie Harden, who had told him that the best thing about leaving welfare was that when her son was asked what his mother did for a living, he could give an answer.

As we watched Clinton walk past the Rose Garden to join us in the Cabinet Room, none of us knew what he would do. He began by asking us to put politics aside and tell him our hopes, fears, and expectations for the bill. The ensuing debate around that table was the most extraordinary we've ever experienced. Everyone sensed the historic significance of the decision the president had to make, and respected the honest differences he had to reconcile. "It was a very moving thing," Clinton himself said afterward. "There was significant disagreement among my advisers about whether this bill should be signed or vetoed, but 100 percent of them recognize the power of the arguments on the other side."

As so often happened, Clinton came up with his own synthesis: Sign the bill, and make Congress restore the immigrant cuts later. It worked. The welfare reform law went on to become the most successful social policy experiment in a generation. Millions left welfare for work, cutting welfare caseloads in half, and people still on welfare were five times more likely to be working. According to the Census Bureau, from 1993 to 2001, poverty among single mothers fell by a stunning one-third, to the lowest rate on record. In the end, Clinton kept both his promises: to restore the immigrant cuts and to make welfare a second chance, not a way of life.

Clinton's decision to sign the welfare bill—like his decision a year earlier to overrule many of his advisers and pursue a balanced budget—was a leap of faith. But he understood what progressives must never forget: We have to reform government in order to save it. After watching welfare, crime, and budget deficits soar in the 1970s, 1980s, and early 1990s, Americans had lost faith in the nation's ability to solve big problems. As Clinton used to say, most people thought the federal government couldn't run a two-car funeral. After he signed welfare reform and the Balanced Budget Act, and brought the country its lowest welfare rolls, sharpest drop in poverty, and first budget surpluses since the 1960s, public confidence in government soared. Clinton knew that you can't be a successful progressive unless people have confidence in government, and people will only have confidence in government if you do the right thing *and make sure it works.*

The secret to victory isn't simply better tactics: stronger turnout, a better ground game, or, so help us, even sharper attack ads. Americans are looking for answers. Everything else is just politics.

CHAPTER 3

OZZIE AND HARRIET DON'T LIVE HERE ANYMORE

History will look back on the past few years as the perfect disaster—a tectonic collision between the old, failed politics and the old, failing economic arrangements. America will have to clear away the rubble to see clearly what we've lost.

The two of us are both in our forties, still young enough to welcome any glimpse in the mirror of gray hair—and the wisdom it might bring. Yet for all practical purposes, the world we grew up in no longer exists. The generations before us built a land of opportunity and certainty, where a job could last a lifetime, one salary could support a family, a house came with only one mortgage, a pension could guarantee a secure retirement, and one generation's decades of hard work and sacrifice could give the next generation a better life. Those certainties were America's security blankets—and one by one, economic and social changes have taken them away.

You can't blame America for being reluctant to let go of

the world of the postwar boom. In real terms, the median family income doubled from 1950 to 1973. It has gone up about 25 percent in the three decades since—with nearly three-quarters of that increase during the Clinton years. Over those past three decades, Americans have done all they could to hold onto the opportunity and security they felt slipping from their grasp. They have worked harder, stayed at work longer, and mortgaged deeper. For many, a middle-class life has come to resemble a game of pickup sticks: As the certainties we used to take for granted are pulled out one after another, Americans strategize how to put off the moment when the whole structure might collapse into a heap.

Politicians don't want to let go of that world either. Each party has promised that era's return, ignored its disappearance, or done both at the same time. When the other side rails against moral decline, and our side mourns the decline of good-paying jobs, what both miss is the cultural and economic confidence of a lost era. We console ourselves with high-definition, flat-screen color TVs, but all our dreams are still in black-and-white. Ozzie and Harriet don't live here anymore, and their children can't stop squabbling about what to do now that they're gone.

What America Has Lost

We're not for rolling the clock back to the 1950s. If we wanted to do that, we would become Republican Supreme

Court nominees. But it's worth reflecting on what we've lost and gained over the last fifty years, as we chart a path through the challenges of the next fifty.

In some respects, the last half century is a story of extraordinary progress. Through bipartisan determination, America won the Cold War. From the Berlin Wall to Latin America, freedom triumphed over oppression. Here at home, we overcame segregation, stood up for civil and equal rights, reduced poverty, and opened the doors of opportunity much wider, even though they are still not open wide enough. We went to the moon, and created the Internet, which joins the telegraph, the telephone, and the television in the pantheon of American inventions that have transformed the human experience. We're the richest, most dynamic, most diverse society on earth—and an economic and military superpower like none before.

And yet for the typical American family, that and four dollars will get you a cup of coffee at Starbucks. The U.S. doesn't feel like such an economic superpower to workers at General Motors, the very symbol of twentieth-century American greatness now struggling just to stay above water in the twenty-first. Striding atop history as the world's sole military superpower is small comfort to Americans who were brought up to think that superpowers won wars and made their people feel safe. Spreading democracy throughout the globe might be more satisfying if Washington weren't making such a mess of it over there and here at home. Although Americans are proud to live in the land of opportunity, we long for the days when those words unabashedly meant the chance to get ahead and earn a better life, not work harder than ever just to keep from losing ground. More than any other people on earth, we're eager to embrace change—but we cling to the innate American belief that change is supposed to bring progress.

Something is wrong when we can be the richest and strongest and still feel as if we're falling behind. That's the great paradox of this new era: The bridge is out between the dynamism of our economy and the success of our people.

That '80s Show

Considering what most Americans are going through, it's criminal that American politics has refused to come to terms with the vast challenges we face. American business leaders understand that in this new era, the first rule is "Change or die." American political leaders may soon discover that the same rule applies to our business as well.

We're still debating a Republican economic theory that was invented thirty years ago, when people danced under disco balls and had never heard of the personal computer. The Republicans' borrow-and-spend approach was built for a world of entirely different economic pressures, and it failed even then. Supply-side tax cuts are the SUVs of American politics: easy to sell, expensive to run, and hopelessly ill-suited for the road to the future.

When the first modern wave of serious economic competition arrived on our shores in the 1980s, in the form of efficient, well-built cars from Germany and Japan, American business quickly realized that we had to improve our game to survive in the new era. Corporations geared up to meet the challenge of moving from an industrial to an information age. Even American automakers, whose resistance to change had let Honda and Toyota steal their customers in the first place, eventually responded by improving the quality—if not the relative fuel efficiency—of cars made in America.

While American business upgraded, downsized, and retooled to meet the global threat, Washington spent the 1980s going in the opposite direction. The Reagan administration pushed huge tax cuts, joined Congress in overspending, ran up huge budget and trade deficits, and added trillions of dollars to the national debt.

Sound familiar? Since the long boom of the last decade came to a halt in this one, the economic challenges America confronts in the world have become increasingly clear. Relentless global competition has forced American companies to cut costs and has made it much harder for them to raise prices. Because employers can't afford to give raises, American incomes failed to go up four years in a row for the first time in history. Now the intense pressure to hold down costs is forcing employers to scale back pensions and health coverage. IBM, one of the best-run companies in America, abandoned its pension plan in favor of defined-contribution 401(k)'s. GM, one of the worst-run companies, is cutting benefits left and right just to keep from going bankrupt.

Every corporation in America is scrambling to survive the competitive squeeze of this new era. Yet, in Washington, Republicans acted as if they were in a 1980s revival. Each year, they passed another round of big tax cuts. Like Reagan, they embraced overspending even as they paid lip service to opposing it. Washington responded to the global challenge with record tax cuts, record budget and trade deficits, trillions of dollars of projected surplus squandered, and trillions more added to the national debt.

Give Republicans credit: At least they're consistent. Whatever else we may say about George W. Bush, we'll be forever in his debt.

Family Troubles

The arrival of a new era may be news to Washington, but it isn't news to the American people. So far, the twenty-first century hasn't turned out quite the way they wanted. The shock of 9/11, and the subsequent realization that the war on terror could last for decades, was bad enough. The disappearance of the old economic certainties has been more gradual, but no less dramatic. According to the Federal Reserve, average household income after inflation fell 2.3 percent between 2001 and 2004. In our nation's capital, where Congress raises its own pay every year, many leaders don't know how the rest of America feels after going four years without a raise. Unlike Congress, ordinary families have to adapt their economic policies to survive. When the economic woes of the 1970s brought a sudden halt to the steady rise in living standards they had grown used to in the 1950s and 1960s, families adapted by sending more women off to work. According to the Families and Work Institute, two-earner families now work an average of ninety-one hours a week—ten hours more than a quarter century ago. Like American business, families have downsized, waiting longer to have children and having fewer when they do.

In this decade, the middle class has already been forced to consider more drastic measures. Thanks to a housing boom and low interest rates, Americans have been able to borrow heavily against their homes. Last year, household debt grew by almost 12 percent, the fastest rate in twenty years. The ratio of debt to after-tax income is twice what it was in 1980. With incomes flat and the costs of many essentials like health care, energy, and college soaring, many families are now forced to tap the one reservoir they have left: their credit cards. Average credit card debt has more than doubled over the past decade, reaching a record $9,312 in 2004.

If families were corporations, they could play out the string a little longer. Indeed, many families are doing just that. A record forty-six million Americans now go without health insurance; nearly twice that many go without coverage at some point during the year. A record two million people filed for bankruptcy last year, despite Washington's mean-spirited and successful effort to make that option more difficult. Just as employers are scaling back pensions, Americans have scaled back saving. Last year, the U.S. had a negative savings rate for the first time since 1933, in the depths of the Great Depression. In fact, the only corporate act of desperation that Americans won't consider is foreign takeover. Of course, by borrowing a quarter trillion dollars from the Chinese, their faithful servants in Washington are trying to arrange that for them.

The average worker experienced another troubling phenomenon: a recovery that didn't raise incomes. Productivity went up, but wages did not. When a jobless economy is followed by a wageless recovery, it's no wonder that most Americans think the economy is off course. They see a growing service sector and a thriving professional class, but they no longer see the economy generating the good old-fashioned middle-class job.

The American economy isn't going down the tubes. The Gross Domestic Product grew 3.3 percent in 2005, and U.S. corporations enjoyed another year of record profits.

But the American middle class finds itself in an untenable position. People can't work much harder than they already do, and they're running out of costs to cut and places to borrow.

Republicans Cut and Run

In the 1990s, Democrats tried to update the nation's policies for this new era. President Clinton persuaded a Democratic Congress in 1993 and a Republican Congress in 1997 to balance the budget for the first time in more than three decades. He showed the country why an aging society with looming obligations couldn't afford to give big tax cuts to those who didn't need them. He challenged his party and the nation to recognize the benefits of expanded trade, but also the urgent need to expand the winner's circle and keep the forces of globalization from undermining the social contract here at home.

Since taking over, Republicans have bloated the federal bureaucracy, passed a drug bill that made the health care sector less efficient, and cultivated a baksheesh culture of special privilege that shelters companies from competition. They've pressed division over progress, because from security to trade to cultural issues, division works to their short-term partisan advantage.

A century ago, philosopher William James argued for stirring a sleepy nation from its slumber by inspiring "the moral equivalent of war." So far this century, Washington's economic neglect, fiscal recklessness, and political bickering have instead offered up the moral equivalent of surrender. Time and time again, Republicans have pontificated that on their watch, America will never "cut and run." But on the key unanswered question of our time—how America can win the fight for our economic lives—the Bush administration cut and ran from the very beginning.

Here is the Republicans' apparent game plan for victory: Make it harder for Americans to afford new skills, while our competitors in China and India do everything they can to make sure their people get the education they need to compete. Allow our competitors to break trade laws with abandon, undermining public support for the trade expansion we need for our economy to grow. Tinker at the margins of issues such as health care and energy that are too big to solve without national leadership. Respond to the first widespread rip in the social contract, the disappearance of pensions, by making Social Security's troubles worse. And as a final burden to middle-class aspirations, abandon the fiscal responsibility that sparked the longest economic boom in American history, and instead saddle us with enormous foreign debt.

When ordinary Americans don't have a way to get ahead anymore, and no longer believe they can leave their children a better life, it's not just another slump or an economic hiccup. It's nearly as profound a shock to our values system as Pearl Harbor, Sputnik, or 9/11.

What Would Lincoln Do?

Throughout American history, the sudden arrival of a new economic era has led—after a painful transition—to a new set of arrangements to meet the era's new challenges. On back-to-back days in July 1862, Abraham Lincoln signed the Pacific Railway Act, to build a route that would transform America's reach from East and West, and the Morrill Act, to charter land-grant colleges that would transform the American people's capacity to get ahead. At the beginning of the twentieth century, when America's booming economy led to an unprecedented concentration of economic power, progressives like Teddy Roosevelt and Woodrow Wilson fought for new institutions to make sure ordinary Americans benefited from that economic power. When the stock market crash and the Great Depression devastated millions of hardworking Americans, FDR wrote new rules to save capitalism from itself and to help people stay afloat and eventually prosper. When millions of American soldiers were headed home from World War II after being out of the workforce for years, FDR signed the GI Bill, which helped create the broad middle class and the long boom of the postwar era.

The challenges of the new economic era we now confront—and the changes we've gone through over the last thirty years—are every bit as wrenching. American companies, American workers, and American families have scrambled to adapt, but American policymakers have not.

On the contrary, the harder and more necessary those changes have become, the less willing the political system has been to make them.

We can't afford to put this off any longer. Our failure to recognize the need for new arrangements is not only costly, but dangerous. When totalitarian communism threatened our security after World War II, Harry Truman and others created new institutions and arrangements to meet the new threat: the United Nations, the North Atlantic Treaty Organization, the containment doctrine, and the Marshall Plan. In the past, our leaders used threats from abroad to unite America and make common cause with allies around the world. Yet today, in a war against a decentralized enemy, when friends are more important than ever, we've abandoned the old arrangements and refused to build others in their place.

We cannot bring back the stability of a more tranquil era. But we ought to be able to make this era secure enough and rewarding enough to restore our faith in progress—and to make that progress happen. America has always been a land of opportunity, not certainty. To keep that alive, we need a new set of arrangements recognizing that the American people have run out of both.

For decades, the conservative laissez-faire theory has been the basic rule of capital: more risk, more reward. In return for accepting more individual risk by agreeing to fewer guarantees and less government protection, Americans were supposed to receive greater individual reward (and lower taxes). In return for the fiscal risk of lowering tax rates, government was supposed to reap the reward of higher revenues. That was the central promise of Bush's Ownership Society: If Americans agreed to a riskier retirement (or health plan or public school system), went the argument, they'd have the chance to earn a higher return.

But a theory designed for capital doesn't seem to work so well for human beings, because markets are a whole lot better at spreading risk than at spreading reward. Ordinary Americans have found themselves with the worst combination of the two, earning less and worrying more. As ordinary Americans watched pensions crumble, health bills soar, and raises evaporate, that Ownership Society seemed like a bad bet: more risk, less reward.

Nor does there seem to be much future for the old liberal hope that we might somehow find a way to live without risk. We can still see the path to equal opportunity, but we cannot (and shouldn't want to) guarantee equal outcomes.

More Work, More Reward

We believe it's time for a new theory based on old American values. Instead of the competing illusions of "more risk, more reward" and "no risk, just reward," we favor two commonsense principles that have helped this nation through tough times before: "more responsibility, less risk," and "more work, more reward."

In the harsh new world, Americans have been led to believe that we must accept trade-offs between our values and our economic interests. But in truth, honoring our values is the best way to advance our economic interests. If we want people to assume more responsibility—for their health, their retirement, their families, and their country—we should make that route safer and more rewarding, not more perilous. If the strength of our economy depends on hard work—on the job and, even earlier, in the classroom—we should make sure that's what our economy and society value most.

Republicans constantly urge Americans to vote their values, which the GOP considers its strong suit. Democrats implore people to vote their pocketbooks, which has long been our strong suit.

But parents don't lie awake at night wondering whether to put food on the table or teach their children right from wrong. The elderly don't choose between affordable prescription drugs for themselves and strong values for their grandchildren. Life isn't a trade-off between opportunity and values. Americans want both, and know that you can't hold onto one without the other.

America was built on what Senator Hillary Clinton has called "the basic bargain." Governor Tom Vilsack calls it "the American Bargain": "When you work hard, you're supposed to get ahead." That bargain built the great middle class and made us the richest country on earth, with the biggest dreams.

By insisting on personal responsibility, rewarding hard work, and reducing individual risk, America can empower people to make the most of change, not fear it. What we miss most about the world of Ozzie and Harriet isn't the quiet streets—it's the quiet, unshakable faith in progress. Americans aren't afraid of sacrifice—to work harder, study longer, serve more. But lately, the only sacrifice we've been asked to make is the one we cannot bear: to give up believing that if we do all those things, the future will be better than the past.

As we set forth in Part 2, The Plan reimagines the social contract because the desire to leave behind a better life *is* our common purpose. In America, progress is not the privilege of the few. It is a faith to be shared by all.

PART TWO

THE PLAN

CHAPTER 4

WHAT'S THE PLAN?

Across party lines, from red states to blue, Americans agree that our country is headed in the wrong direction. As a nation, we know we're not doing enough to win two wars America cannot afford to lose—one with economic competitors that could undermine our standard of living, the other with terrorists out to destroy our way of life.

With stakes that high, the question that matters most is the one our political system seems least inclined to answer: What are we going to do about it?

Too often, those of us in Washington never get around to discussing what to do because we're so busy searching for someone to blame. We don't have far to look.

We will never make progress by whining about what we're against. It is high time to say what we're for, what we stand for, and above all, what we plan to do.

America faces three great, urgent challenges. We need a new social contract for economic growth that enables Americans to get ahead again. We need a new strategy to make America safe again. And we need a new sense of patriotism and responsibility that unites us in common purpose again.

In the next several chapters, we offer many ideas about how to meet those challenges. We don't have all the answers—and we hope that you will tell us yours—but we do know this: America can rise to every one of these challenges if we hold ourselves to a clear, ambitious vision.

At other turning points in our history, our leaders debated and invented the new norms and institutions we needed to carry on as a nation. Their ideas made new eras possible. At the beginning of the last century, Theodore Roosevelt busted trusts and built new institutions to keep markets from crushing the little man. At the end of that century, Bill Clinton eliminated the budget deficit and reformed broken programs like welfare in order to save government from itself. During the Great Depression, when capitalism and government alike were failing, FDR stepped forward to save both.

At the beginning of the twentieth century, the U.S. faced a series of new and difficult challenges: an unprecedented concentration of wealth; the transition from an agrarian to an industrial economy, and, with it, rapid migration from rural to urban areas; an enormous influx of immigrants; and with America's emergence as a military power, the need to define our role in the world and how we would use that power. As we begin a new century, we find ourselves confronting a similar and equally daunting list: an accelerating concentration of wealth and opportunity; the transition from an industrial to an information economy, and, with it, rapid migration from urban to suburban and exurban areas; another surge of immigrants; and with America's emergence as the sole military superpower, the need once again to define our role in the world, and to sort out how best to put our power to good purpose.

In a 1910 speech to Civil War veterans in Osawatomie, Kansas, Theodore Roosevelt responded to the challenges of his day by calling for "a New Nationalism, without which we cannot hope to deal with new problems." As Roosevelt said in that speech:

> At every stage, and under all circumstances, the essence of the struggle is to equalize opportunity, destroy privilege, and give to the life and citizenship of every individual the highest possible value. . . . We work in a spirit of broad and far-reaching nationalism when we work for what concerns people as a whole. We are all Americans. Our common interests are as broad as the continent.

A century later, we must be just as inventive, practical, and fearless in addressing the challenges of our time, with a new patriotism that brings us together again in a common mission. We propose a new bargain between the people and their country—a social contract to equip Americans for the twenty-first century and unite us in higher national purpose. The terms of this bargain may be new, but the bedrock principle is not: You do your part, and your government, your company, and your country will do theirs.

We believe that individuals have a responsibility to make the most of their own lives, and that government has a responsibility to make sure they have the opportunity, the security, and the tools to do so.

We believe that this opportunity and security for all—with special privilege for none—is America's special mission.

We believe there can be no security without responsibility, no responsibility without opportunity, no opportunity without a new trust in the promise of American life. A new bargain between the people and their country must offer Americans more of the opportunity and security we remember, in return for more responsibilities that for too long we forgot.

America has plenty of unfinished business, and all of the reforms we'd like to see—some of which appear in this book—would make for a very long list. But if we're going to turn the country around, we need a bold agenda that can be counted off on one hand:

1. A new social contract—universal citizen service, universal college access, universal retirement savings, and universal children's health care—that

makes clear what you can do for your country and what your country can do for you.

2. A return to fiscal responsibility and an end to corporate welfare as we know it.
3. Tax reform to help those who aren't wealthy build wealth.
4. A new strategy to use all America's strengths to win the war on terror.
5. A Hybrid Economy that cuts America's gasoline consumption in half over the next decade.

Each of these ideas represents a serious effort to address America's most pressing national challenges. Each of them marks a clean break with the status quo, yet all are practical ideas that can be passed and put into action right away.

Above all, these ideas recognize that the world has changed, and so must we. The economic arrangements Americans depend on have stayed the same for generations. America's social contract was designed for the 1930s. Our safety net was built for the 1960s. Our preparations for the twenty-first century came to a halt at the end of the twentieth.

The chapters that follow describe these ideas in depth. But for those who—like us—are impatient for change, here's a shorthand version of The Plan:

THE PLAN

A NEW SOCIAL CONTRACT, OR WHAT YOU CAN DO FOR YOUR COUNTRY AND WHAT YOUR COUNTRY CAN DO FOR YOU

THE economy of the twenty-first century demands new skills and will require all of us to live up to new responsibilities. We believe that four mutual obligations that follow should represent the first terms of a new contract between the people and their country.

Universal Citizen Service

If you forget everything else you read in these pages, please remember this: The Plan starts with you. If your leaders aren't challenging you to do your part, they aren't doing theirs. We need a real Patriot Act that brings out the patriot in all of us by establishing, for the first time, an ethic of universal citizen service. All Americans between the ages of eighteen and twenty-five should be asked to serve their country by going through three months of basic civil defense training and community service. This is not a draft—nor is it military. Young people will be trained not as soldiers, but simply as citizens who understand their responsibilities in the event of a natural disaster, an epidemic, or a terrorist attack. Universal citizen service will bring Americans of every background together to make America safer and more united in common national purpose.

Universal College Access

We must make a college degree as universal as a high school diploma. More than ever, America's success depends on what we can learn. We have an education system built in the last century, with a school year left over from the century before that. In this new era, college will be the greatest engine of opportunity for our society and our economy. Just as Abraham Lincoln gave land grants to endow our great public universities, we will give the states tuition grants to make college free for those willing to work, serve, and excel.

Universal Retirement Savings

From now on, every job ought to come with a 401(k). An aging society cannot afford to keep saving less and risking more. We need new means to create wealth, based on the needs and responsibilities of twenty-first-century employees and employers. Employers should be required to offer 401(k)'s, and workers will be enrolled unless they choose otherwise. If they switch jobs, they can take these accounts with them. When their paycheck goes up, so will their savings. Instead of a workforce in which only half the workers have retirement savings plans, every American will have one.

Universal Children's Health Care

We need to cut the cost of health care so that every business can afford it and every child in America at last can get it. We can save hundreds of billions by adopting electronic medical records, rewarding outcomes instead of procedures, providing incentives for personal responsibility, and starting a National Cure Center to cure chronic diseases. As we achieve those savings, we should use them to give small businesses access to the same health plans as members of Congress—and to make sure all parents in America have the responsibility and the means to obtain health insurance for their children.

A RETURN TO FISCAL RESPONSIBILITY AND AN END TO CORPORATE WELFARE AS WE KNOW IT

WE'LL never be able to build a new social contract if we don't repair the broken contract between the American people and their leaders. We can only achieve universal service, college, pensions, and children's health care if we're willing to cut and invest to pay for it. The place to start is by ending corporate welfare and the Hack-ridden government that fuels it.

TAX REFORM TO HELP THOSE WHO AREN'T WEALTHY BUILD WEALTH

AMERICANS shouldn't have to start rich to get rich, and the tax code shouldn't punish them for going to work or for being members of the middle class. We need tax reform that puts a lid on middle-class taxes and helps every American build the pillars of the American Dream: raising a family, buying a home, paying for college, and saving for retirement.

A NEW STRATEGY TO WIN THE WAR ON TERROR

WE need to use all the tools of American power to make our country safe. America must lead the world's fight against the spread of evil and totalitarianism, but we must stop trying to win that battle on our own. We should reform and strengthen multilateral institutions for the twenty-first century, not walk away from them. We need to fortify the military's "thin green line" around the world by adding to the U.S. Special Forces and the Marines, and expanding the U.S. Army by 100,000 more troops. We should give all our troops a new GI Bill to come home to. Finally, we must protect the homeland and our civil liberties by creating a new domestic counterterrorism force like Britain's MI5.

A HYBRID ECONOMY THAT CUTS AMERICA'S GASOLINE USE IN HALF

AMERICA needs to usher in the Hybrid Economy, a new era of energy efficiency and innovation that can save the auto industry and the planet at the same time. We need a sweeping campaign to develop new energy technologies, which can be the job engine of the twenty-first century and our nation's response to the threat of climate change. We can cut our use of gasoline in half over the next decade by accelerating energy research and by embracing a technology that already exists—the plug-in hybrid, which in combination with alternative fuels has the potential to deliver a hundred miles per gallon. Instead of sending tens of billions a year to support corrupt regimes whose neglect and corruption keep terrorism alive, we'll end our dependence on a dangerous region that harbors many who wish us great harm.

CHAPTER 5

ASKED NOT: Universal Citizen Service

No one should take seriously a political platform that promises more and expects less, any more than a diet book that says eating more and exercising less is the way to lose weight. John Kennedy was right: A nation is defined not by what it does for its citizens, but by what it asks of them.

In the stale political debate of recent years, some in Washington have given Americans a stirring choice between programs and tax cuts. The parties are divided over which answer will do more damage, but neither approach exactly offers a beeline to greatness.

Many on both sides start from a flawed premise that voters are looking for one promissory note or another: If you can't pander to the one you love, then pander to the one you're with.

The road ahead is steep. The challenges of the next fifty years will be greater than the ones we overcame in the last fifty. We're the sole superpower and biggest target in a world where the capacity for evil is more decentralized than ever before. After a century of unparalleled economic progress, the U.S. now faces competitors in China and India that have the potential to eclipse us if we are complacent. For years, we have worked to remake the world in our image by spreading the gospel of democracy, freedom, and capitalism. Doing so has been and continues to be in our national interest. But we should not forget: The more the world copies our strengths, the harder we must work to hone those strengths ourselves.

Half a century ago, Americans were jolted out of complacency by a loud, rising threat from the Soviet Union. The Russians launched the first satellite into orbit and threatened to bury us in the battle for hearts and minds around the world. We didn't see it at the time, but the Soviets did us a great favor, spurring us to bolster our technological and military superiority, and to get serious about shoring up our democracy.

This time the race may not be as easy for us to see. But there can be no doubt: This is our generation's *Sputnik* moment. If we don't rise to the economic challenge, our independence will be endangered and our standard of living will decline. If we don't rise to the security challenge, our way of life will never be the same. And we will always regret it if we pass up this historic opportunity to raise our sights as a nation.

Every great president has tried to lift the nation up. In

the wake of Pearl Harbor, FDR transformed a struggling, isolationist nation into the greatest economic and military power on earth, launched the most dramatic explosion of middle-class opportunity in history, and instilled a spirit of sacrifice and responsibility we prize sixty years later. Three years after *Sputnik* had left Americans wondering whether the Soviet Union might prevail in space and perhaps in the Cold War, JFK restored their faith more by calling on all Americans to ask what they could do for their country than by promising to put a man on the moon.

The contrast between those presidencies and this latest one is stark and disheartening. Following 9/11, Bush corroded America's economic engine, concentrated wealth, and ran up debts that will force our children to sacrifice for sixty years hence. Handed the chance to make history, he made us go broke instead.

Now, a great nation must find in us the greatness that George Bush never sought. The world changed on 9/11, and America must change with it. It is time to ask Americans in all walks of life to give something back.

The Case for Universal Citizen Service

Every citizen needs to understand and accept the essence of the American bargain: *Each of us has to do his or her part.* While the rights of citizenship are explicit in our Constitution, the implicit responsibilities are every bit as crucial.

For our radical experiment in freedom to work, we must prize responsibilities as well as rights, and never presume to do for people what they can do for themselves.

After 9/11, both parties in Washington spent countless hours debating a law called the Patriot Act, which gave federal authorities new powers to police terrorism. We're all for giving law enforcement the tools to do its job; the two of us helped write legislation to do just that (which the Republican Congress largely rejected) after domestic terrorists blew up the federal building in Oklahoma City in 1995. We have no problem with spying on terrorists, here or elsewhere. Indeed, as we'll explain later, we believe the U.S. should strengthen its domestic counterterrorism capacity in a way that also safeguards our freedoms.

Our problem with the Patriot Act is simpler: It doesn't have much to do with patriotism. We want the government to be aggressive in protecting us from terrorists. But we want a government that's just as serious about challenging us as citizens. Americans' role in the war on terror is not simply to be waving flags on the sidelines.

It's time for a real Patriot Act that brings out the patriot in all of us. We propose universal civilian service for every young American. Under this plan, all Americans between the ages of eighteen and twenty-five will be asked to serve their country by going through three months of basic training, civil defense preparation, and community service.

This is not a draft. We repeat: This is not a draft. It's not military either. We're not asking young people to be soldiers, but to be citizens—ready to respond to the nation's needs here at home.

The idea of universal civilian service may not be popular everywhere in our party. Some Republicans will squeal about individual freedom, forgetting their own rhetoric that freedom isn't being free. But universal service is the right thing to do, and our country will be stronger for it.

Here's how it would work. Young people will know that between the ages of eighteen and twenty-five, the nation will enlist them for three months of civilian service. They'll be asked to report for basic civil defense training in their state or community, where they will learn what to do in the event of biochemical, nuclear, or conventional attack; how to assist others in an evacuation; how to respond when a levee breaks or we're hit by a natural disaster. These young people will be available to address their communities' most pressing needs.

For those willing to make a longer commitment to their community and country, we will dramatically expand access to AmeriCorps, which provides college assistance in return for extended service.

In the 1990s, Bill Clinton and the late Eli Segal launched AmeriCorps, which has given more than 400,000 young people the chance to serve their country. After 9/11, even President Bush briefly proposed a modest increase in AmeriCorps, only to let House conservatives scale it back. At one revealing point, the administration stopped awarding AmeriCorps scholarships because, like the rest of compassionate conservatism, the program ran out of money.

By asking every young American to serve, universal civilian service will strengthen America in three vital ways.

First, it will provide real, lasting security benefits. We shouldn't kid ourselves—the war on terror won't be over anytime soon. The Cold War lasted nearly half a century; what some call this "long war" could go on for decades. If that's the case, citizens are going to have to get tougher, smarter, and stronger. The best antidote to fear is preparation. In World War II, cities and towns turned out the lights and pulled down the shades for blackout drills. We grew up in the Cold War listening to weekly air raid sirens. Yet today, most Americans have no clue what to do in the event of a nuclear, chemical, or biological attack. The Department of Homeland Security hasn't told us. Training young people in civilian defense—and enlisting them to train and inform others—will pay immediate practical dividends. America will feel safer, and *be* safer.

Second, universal civilian service may be just what we need to save the volunteer army and *avoid* a draft. In the 2000 campaign, George W. Bush and Dick Cheney promised the military that "help is on the way." Then the Bush administration steadily depleted and abused both the armed forces and the National Guard and the Reserves.

Sending young soldiers into battle without sufficient body armor and extending tours without relief took a heavy toll on recruiting back home. Universal service will not compel anyone to serve in the military, but it may increase the pool of young people willing to volunteer for military service. Joining the military never crosses the minds of many young people today. They may not even know anyone who's considering it. Through universal civilian service, millions of young people will meet others who have served or plan to serve, and will no longer view duty to their country as someone else's job.

Third, and most important, universal service will give young people a chance early in their lives to look past differences of race, class, creed, and region, and to see themselves and one another first and foremost as Americans. We are the most diverse nation on earth. To lead the world in this century, we must make the most of that great strength, not let our differences become a burden. The U.S. military is an extraordinary example of differences giving way to national purpose. Civilian service can do the same, bringing people of vastly different backgrounds together to serve side by side and find common ground with a common purpose.

The Duty We Owe One Another

Service to country may sound like an old-fashioned answer to the challenges of a new millennium when we fight wars with smart bombs and use electronic sensors to deter terrorist attacks. Why should the U.S. invest in universal service when we don't even have universal health care, or broadband, or pensions?

We need to meet those responsibilities, too, but we ought to start with our common responsibilities as citizens. For of all the competitive advantages America enjoys in the world, our greatest untapped advantage is that we've always expected more of ourselves than have the citizens of any other country. After World War II, Harry Truman proposed universal military training to show the Soviets our mettle. Today, none question our military prowess, but universal nonmilitary service would show friend and foe alike how much we are united.

In a diverse world of fewer and fewer borders, holding a nation together will be both more difficult and more important. For America, where we pride ourselves on both the strength of our common identity and the diversity of our backgrounds, the new era poses an opportunity and a challenge. The London bombings by homegrown terrorists in July 2005 foreshadow the challenge we and every other country must face: how to make people set aside other differences and see themselves as citizens first. The U.S. should do more to instill a sense of civic duty, if for no other reason than that Americans are good at it—and will need to be.

Service to country is a great, enduring American success story, from the Minutemen who died at Lexington and

Concord to the firefighters who rushed up the stairs of the World Trade Center. All the cynicism about modern politics has not diminished Americans' idealism about service.

Ours is not the only way to make service a common experience: In the *Washington Monthly,* Paul Glastris and Charlie Moskos have urged requiring a year of service as a condition of college. Other nations, from Israel to Switzerland to Scandinavia, have required service for years. The French abandoned the idea a decade ago, and now watch their young people riot in the streets.

When John Kennedy challenged young people to join the Peace Corps, he awakened the idealism of an entire generation. Universal service has the power to be the next generation's Peace Corps. In fact, it should be even bigger.

When millions were called to serve America in World War II, this proved to be a great equalizer. After the war, our country built the largest middle class in history—and a few years later, the nation began the steady march for civil rights. Today, we desperately need again the chance to forge common bonds. Many aspects of our lives—neighborhoods, schools, popular culture, political affiliation—are simply not the common experiences they once were, or could be again. Yet through universal service we can still give every young person the common experience that means the most: that of being an American.

We begin The Plan with responsibility for a reason: That is where a nation begins. Our future depends on renewing that bargain. In America, opportunity and responsibility go hand in hand.

CHAPTER 6

TOGA PARTY: Universal College Access

When we went off to college in the late 1970s, America's economic position in the world never crossed our minds. Even if it had, we couldn't have figured out what studying Dickens or ballet had to do with the price of oil from OPEC. But when our children head off to college in a few years, we will be thinking of America's place in the world. The U.S. knows now what had not yet become clear a quarter century ago: Nothing will strengthen America's economy more over the long haul than to send every young American to college.

Over the last century, college became the centerpiece of the American Dream and the door to the middle class. Millions of soldiers who came home from World War II and went to college on the GI Bill of Rights turned America into a middle-class country. Parents have always understood the magic of a college degree. They scrimp, save, and sacrifice to send their children to college because it's the ticket to a better life.

Today, we know the Information Age depends on knowledge. Yet, although the rest of the world has moved on, American expectations have not changed enough. Just as the nation made high school universal in another era, we must make college—the key tool of the twenty-first century—universal in this one.

Education brought about two of the most important economic and social developments of the twentieth century. First, high school became universal. A century ago, about 5 percent of Americans graduated from high school. Today, 85 percent of adults over the age of twenty-five have a high school degree. Second, the GI Bill sent more than two million World War II veterans to college, helping spark the greatest expansion of the middle class in history. As Peter Shapiro wrote in *A History of National Service in America*, the U.S. considered the GI Bill so important to America's economic future that by 1949, we were dedicating nearly 1 percent of Gross National Product to pay for it.

If college was an attractive ideal in the Industrial Economy, it has become a virtual necessity in the Information Age. In a global, information economy, college is central to whether individuals—and nations—can get ahead.

Even in our youth, Milton-Bradley's "Game of Life" awarded higher salaries to players who chose to go to college. The wealth gap begins with an education gap. Today, the gulf between college and high school graduates is greater than ever. College grads earn an average of

$51,000 a year, compared with $28,000 a year for those who only finish high school. A current high school senior who goes on to finish college will earn over a million dollars more by her fiftieth high school reunion.

According to a 2006 study by the Federal Reserve, the average net worth of a high school dropout is $20,000. For families headed by a college graduate, the average is $226,000. Unless we close the education gap, our other efforts to increase wealth and opportunity will come up short.

When Americans go to college, they're not the only ones whose bottom line will benefit. Colleges, universities, and the minds and innovations they produce are vital to a nation's success in the global economy. In recent years, America's universities have helped spawn entire new industries, from biomedical research to nanotechnology to Web search engines. We depend on our colleges to turn out the innovators, engineers, and skilled thinkers who will keep America ahead of the pack.

College makes all sorts of dreams possible, but for most Americans, it is still a dream denied or deferred. Although the U.S. is justly proud of having the finest system of colleges and universities in the world, the rest of the world seems to understand the value of college better than we do. America was once first in the world in college enrollment. Now we rank ninth. We're also the only industrialized country *not* to increase its college graduation rate in the last twenty years. India produces about twice as many college grads each year as the U.S.; China graduates three times as many as we do—and their universities are becoming world-class.

College is vital to our individual economic success, our collective economic survival, and, above all, our faith in a better future. The social contract will be null and void without it. Yet instead of spreading this miracle of college, Washington let it be priced out of most Americans' reach. According to the College Board, public tuition at a four-year college went up more than 50 percent over the last five years. Yet the Bush administration pushed the largest cut in college aid in history, and failed to keep its promise to significantly increase Pell Grants. Tuition at a four-year public college now costs about $5,500 a year. At private universities, the average is more than $21,000.

At that price, what used to be the door to the middle class is being slammed in the middle class's face. According to Thomas G. Mortenson of the Institute for the Study of Opportunities in Higher Education, students from families earning more than $90,000 have a 50 percent chance of getting a college degree by age twenty-four. The odds of a student whose family earns less than $35,000 getting a degree are one in seventeen. A 2004 Century Foundation study of the nation's 146 most selective colleges by Anthony P. Carnevale and Stephen J. Rose showed that the gap at the most prestigious institutions is even worse. As Richard D. Kahlenberg puts it, "Wandering around one of the nation's selective campuses, you are 25 times as likely to run into a rich student as a poor one." Citing another study of students with comparable ability but different incomes, Kahlenberg writes, "The dumb, rich kids had as much chance of going to college as the smart, poor ones." If a nation is dumb enough to deny anyone the chance to go to college, it won't stay rich for long.

Closing the College Gap

The main reason young people don't go to college—or don't finish—is cost. For starters, we need to get rid of the red tape in their way. The tax code is littered with well-intentioned but confusing and often contradictory education provisions, with different rules, definitions, and limits. We should simplify the tax code by replacing the five major existing education tax incentives—the Hope Scholarship, the Lifetime Learning Credit, the deduction for higher-education expenses, the exclusion of employer-provided education benefits, and the exclusion for qualified tuition reductions—with a single $3,000-a-year refundable credit for four years of college and two years of graduate school. If we want young people to go to college, they shouldn't have to stop first at H&R Block.

Second, we need to keep colleges from pricing us out of the global economic competition. As Michael Dannenberg of the New America Foundation has suggested, we should pass a truth-in-tuition law that requires colleges to set multiyear tuition and fee levels so that those in each incoming freshman class know in advance exactly what their degree will cost them.

Most important, we should take the billions we can save by lending directly to students instead of subsidizing banks, and use the money to provide Tuition Grants to states. Like the land grants of the nineteenth century, which gave the states federal land to endow public colleges, these Tuition Grants would enable states to offer free or low-cost tuition to students who work their way through school, excel in class, or commit to careers in critical professions. According to the Institute for Higher Education Policy, states need the help: In 1980, half the funding for public colleges and universities came from state and local governments, which in 2000 were able to provide just a third of the money. Students and parents have been left to pick up the slack through sharply higher tuitions.

The national government has a responsibility to make two to four years of college as universal as four years of high school. Our goal is to challenge everyone to go to college, and make it affordable for everyone to do so. In the 1990s, AmeriCorps linked college aid with national service. In the years to come, with the strength of our economy on the line, going to college will itself be a form of national service.

The Other Dropout Problem

If we're going to send more young people to college and spend more to help them pay for it, we need to hold colleges accountable for producing more graduates as a result. From federal student loan programs to state university budgets, taxpayers make a substantial investment in the college system, and they deserve to know they're getting a good return. The Education Trust, the preeminent think tank focused on closing the achievement gap in American education, estimates that more than half a million students drop out of four-year colleges every year. According to Kevin Carey in a 2004 Education Trust report, dropping out of college is not a new problem, but in a global economy, its consequences are more severe. In decades past, Carey writes, "Lack of success in college was seen as an individual disappointment, not a national dilemma." Now, he says, it's our problem:

> Low college graduation rates are something our economy can no longer afford and our society must no longer tolerate. As a nation, we've been profligate with our aspiring college students. Every year, hundreds of thousands of young people leave our higher education system unsuccessfully, burdened with large student loans that must be repaid, but without the benefit of the wages that a college degree provides. These students are disproportionately low-income

and people of color. For many, going to college was their first, best, and last opportunity for real economic mobility and success.

Colleges may enjoy cashing the checks of incoming freshmen, but the rest of us would prefer to watch a parade of graduating seniors. And colleges can do a great deal to help make sure that people who start college stick with it and finish. The Education Trust found that colleges serving identical populations had widely different graduation rates, depending on whether the institutions made a significant effort to address the dropout problem. Louisiana Tech, for example, was able to increase its graduation rate from 35 percent to 55 percent in just five years.

We should require colleges to disclose more complete data on graduation rates and student progress. If graduation rates are chronically low, colleges should have to carry out a concrete plan to increase them. States should look at the accountability system in Britain, which holds back a portion of colleges' public funding until students actually graduate.

Lifetime Education and Turning America's Public Schools Around

Of course, education is no longer just for young people. We also need to provide twenty-first-century tools for people already in the workplace. The new $3,000 tax credit for college should be made available to any worker at any age who wants to upgrade his or her skills at an accredited institution. We should expect companies to train all their workers, not just executives. And instead of waiting to retrain workers until after workers have been displaced by global competition, we should provide lifelong training to give every American an economic insurance policy.

Finally, if we want more and better college graduates, we need to strengthen and reform our system of public education in elementary and secondary school. Once again, the Bush administration left a mess to clean up. With the No Child Left Behind Act, the education disparity the president most wanted to close was not the achievement gap, but the gap in Republicans' poll numbers on education.

A decade ago, Republicans tried to abolish the Department of Education. The Bush administration took a different route: running the department badly. Bush invested far too little in the reforms that would make No Child Left Behind succeed: more and better teachers, better (not just more) tests, and state efforts to turn failing schools around. His Education Department hired image consultants and gave conservative commentator Armstrong Williams a $240,000 slush payment to editorialize in favor of the law. Washington bureaucrats ignored sensible suggestions from states, schools, and teachers, setting back educational accountability and reform, rather than advancing them.

It is time to revive the standards movement with the reforms Bush forgot: attracting topflight teachers by rewarding them for performance, not just credentials, and by offering higher pay to teach in high-need areas and subjects; expanding preschool and after-school; and providing more choices within the public school system. Each of these reforms has opponents on one side of the aisle or the other, but strong support from principals, teachers, and parents.

And we need to transform the weakest link in our educational system: high school. A nation with many of the best colleges on earth must no longer tolerate having some of the worst high schools. The saddest indictment of our school system is that the longer American students spend in it, the farther they fall behind students in other countries. In fourth grade, our students are near the top in reading and math; by eighth grade, they start falling behind; by the time they finish high school, they are far back in the pack.

As former Virginia governor Mark Warner told the 2005 National Education Summit on High Schools, "We can't keep explaining to our nation's parents or business leaders or college faculties why these kids can't do the work." More flexibility and resources in return for tougher accountability and rigor is the right formula for education reform at any level. But that formula has scarcely been tried in high schools, where it is best suited and would have the greatest impact. We need high schools that are smaller and more demanding. All secondary-school math and science teachers should have a degree in the field they teach. Because students do better and stay in school longer when their courses mean something, we should offer a rigorous curriculum that is aligned with the skills that universities demand. By challenging high school seniors to take courses at community colleges or online, we can make the senior year of high school feel more like the freshman year in college.

Also, by the time American students are seniors, they have spent two years less time in school than their counterparts in our major competitors. Our current school year wasn't designed for the Information Age or even the Industrial Era; it's a remnant of our agrarian past. We need to increase the amount of time young people spend learning—by lengthening the school day, extending the school year, and keeping young people engaged in learning over the course of the summer. The three-month-long summer break sets the learning clock back twice that long. We should require summer school for those who fall behind—as Chicago has done—and insist that all students spend at least as much of their summers doing online exercises in basic skills like reading and math as they spend sending one another instant messages.

As the Hart-Rudman Commission concluded, "The inadequacy of our system of research and education poses a greater threat to U.S. national security over the next quarter century than any potential conventional war."

From now on, children across this country ought to grow up knowing—from their parents, their teachers, their neighbors, and their president—that education is not only the greatest opportunity America has to offer, but their patriotic duty. When the Soviets launched *Sputnik* into space in the 1950s, President Eisenhower challenged America to put education first. The educational threat from our competitors today is far greater than any we faced then. America's young people shouldn't be kept waiting any longer.

CHAPTER 7

WHO WANTS TO BE A MILLIONAIRE?: Universal Retirement Savings

America is a land of great aspirations. We dream of a better life, even in our frothiest entertainments. Look at some of the most popular television shows of recent years: *Who Wants to Be a Millionaire?*, a quiz show in which the winner gets a million dollars; a copycat show called *Who Wants to Marry a Multi-Millionaire?*, in which the winner dumped her new husband and was immediately offered the chance to pose nude on the Internet for a million dollars; *Survivor,* in which one year the last surviving member went to jail for failing to pay taxes on his winnings of a million dollars; and this year's model, *American Inventor,* in which thousands of people created wacky new products in hopes of capturing the grand prize—you guessed it, a million dollars. Astute observers of our culture will note that if there's one thing Americans still find missing in their lives, it's a million dollars.

Unfortunately, the everyday lives of most Americans are a reality show without that fairy-tale ending. Their fantasies have kept up with inflation, but their assets have not.

Americans have made some progress. Half a century ago, only 55 percent of Americans owned their own homes. Today, after a remarkable increase in the 1990s, a record 69 percent of households are homeowners. The popularity of 401(k)'s, the demystification of investment, and the stock market boom of the 1990s have helped make Americans investors as well. In 1989, less than a third of American households owned stock. Today, about half do.

Yet, in many respects, Americans look at the last few decades and feel more as if they're losing ground or struggling to hold onto what they have. In the last twenty-five years, the median price of a new home has nearly quadrupled. All over the country, the cost of housing has sent the middle class on an exodus to the exurbs. Over the same period, according to the Congressional Budget Office, the average after-tax income of the top 1 percent of households has more than doubled. The middle fifth of the population has seen its income go up less than one percentage point a year.

Although many Americans own more than they used to—bigger houses, more stocks—the demands on their nest eggs have grown much faster than the nest eggs themselves. Life expectancy increased by thirty years in the last century, and the number of Americans living to age one hundred is projected to increase sixfold in the next twenty-five years. Yet the percentage of Americans with retirement security is dwindling fast. Americans are far more likely to set money aside for college than a generation ago, but the cost of college is going up even faster.

Over the years, Americans have learned the hassles of homeownership—you're on your own when the roof leaks, the pipes break, and the motor on the washing machine burns out. In this decade, we've learned that stock ownership is not always what it's cracked up to be either. Hot stocks like Enron and WorldCom vanish overnight. Markets plunge on events halfway across the globe. The world offers a dizzying array of investment choices, which most of us see as an exponential rise in the odds that we will pick the wrong one. Investing is a boon for those who don't need the money. For those with little to spare, the market can be a very bumpy ride.

In large part, global markets are to blame for another cruel paradox: At the same time that ownership is becoming a dicier proposition, it has become an absolutely essential one. The old saying "It takes money to make money" has never been more true. According to the CBO, the top 1 percent of households owns almost twice as much of the nation's corporate wealth as it did fifteen years ago. Combined with the tax policies of the Bush administration, the pressures of the modern economy—such as global competition and productivity growth—dramatically reduced the return on labor and increased the return on capital. For the typical worker, a technological breakthrough could unfortunately mean fewer hours and a smaller paycheck. For an owner, the same breakthrough could mean higher profits. In this economy, if you're a worker but not an owner, you're probably falling behind and you may never catch up.

There may be ways to slow or mitigate these trends, but it would be foolhardy to expect to reverse them. In the narrowest sense, George Bush was right: We're going to be an ownership society. In some ways, America has always been an ownership society. Breaking away from a country of kings and dukes, the Founders were firm believers in private property. The Homestead Act of 1862 gave pioneers 160 acres if they agreed to live there for five years. Although we've always had a healthy suspicion of speculation—with good reason—Americans have long been believers in investing time, effort, and money toward the prospect of better days. What Bush got wrong is the kind of ownership society America should be.

More Ownership *and* More Security

Ownership must be an even more essential part of the social contract in this century than it has been in the last two. Our most fundamental values—upward mobility, opportunity for all, the pursuit of happiness in a nation of equals—depend on whether every citizen has a stake in the future. To achieve that dream, we need to give all Americans the chance to own their destiny, and to make sure the benefits of ownership come with a warranty.

Republicans proposed just the opposite—a plan to help the few own the most. They rewrote the tax code to reward wealth over work and capital over labor, and they laid out ill-advised schemes to overhaul Social Security, health insurance, and savings policy. For the vast majority of Americans with few or no assets, Bush's Ownership Society reneged on existing promises and sold them a reduced and riskier stake.

Bill Clinton's proposal for Universal Savings Accounts on top of Social Security represented a serious step to ownership and retirement security. Under his plan, the U.S. would set aside the surplus to reduce the national debt and put Social Security back on a sound long-term footing. In addition, every American could set up a universal account, matched on a sliding scale by the government. Shoring up Social Security would increase national savings, and universal accounts would increase private savings. The result: more ownership and more security at the same time.

Bush's plan for private Social Security accounts, by contrast, offered limited and illusory ownership in return for greater risk. Because Bush squandered the surplus on tax cuts, his only nod toward long-term solvency was to propose that benefits be cut. To pay for private accounts, Bush had to dig the country still deeper into debt—an unlikely way to strengthen the nation's long-term finances. What great riches could Americans expect after all that trouble? An uncertain account that might lose money, and if it happened to make gains, would have to use some of them to pay Social Security back. Whatever was left in the private account would have to be converted into an annuity that would provide the recipient a monthly check, in all likelihood no larger than what the recipient had lost because of cuts in Social Security.

In the end, even congressional Republicans couldn't run away fast enough from Bush's boneheaded Social Security plan. Other items in his ownership agenda bore the same fatal flaws, from Health Savings Accounts, a great deal so long as you're not sick and need health care, to Lifetime Savings Accounts, designed to prompt further saving by people who already do it.

Like so much of his agenda, Bush's Ownership Society went awry for a reason: It was a political vision, not a practical one. In part, Republicans saw a chance to bury the New Deal and try life without a safety net. At the same time, Karl Rove and company wanted to buy the love of aspirational middle-class voters who might be open to risk for the right reward. "Most people who are investors tend to vote Republican," Republican National Committee Chair Ken Mehlman told the *Washington Post* in January 2005. "This creates conditions under which voters are more likely to support politicians who are pro-growth, pro-ownership, pro-free market." Unfortunately for Republicans, bad policy turned out to be bad politics. The return on Bush's political investment has been all negative, and some Republicans may well go belly up.

The Bush plan only exacerbated unsettling trends of the global economy. Most Americans have enough risk in their lives; they don't need more of it. The first step to strengthening Social Security is to help people begin building a comfortable nest egg outside Social Security. When only half of Americans have retirement savings, it's impossible to lay the foundation for ensuring the long-term solvency of Social Security. Once we restore people's confidence in their own savings—and stop rattling their confidence by piling up debt in Washington—we will be able to make bipartisan progress on Social Security.

A social contract for this century must address three challenges that did not exist in the last one. First, we're not getting any younger. An aging society needs to plan now for living longer, to take advantage of the fact that unlike many great social challenges, getting older is a welcome and entirely predictable problem. Second, we can't work any harder. The New Deal was built for a labor-intensive economy—where it was enough to seek higher, more predictable wages, not greater, more widespread wealth. In today's world, we must have both. Third, we need markets that work. From trust-busting to the Securities and Exchange Commission, both Roosevelts demanded reforms and institutions that helped save capitalism from itself. In a fiercely competitive global economy, we need capitalism more than ever—which is why we must save global capitalism from itself.

The genius of the Social Security System, when FDR signed it into law in 1935, was that in the midst of crisis, the country was willing to strengthen itself for the long haul. Today, our challenge ought to be much easier by comparison. We're a rich, successful country that is living longer and would like to make the most of those years. The aging of America will lead to significant changes in our society, and to get ready all we really need is to see it coming.

At the moment, we're doing just the opposite—looking in the mirror like Dorian Gray, instead of at the aging portrait that is hidden away. For the last six years, Washington has spent as if there's no tomorrow. The cost of making the Bush tax cuts permanent will be three times larger than the size of the Social Security shortfall over the next seventy-five years. In fact, just the cost of the tax cuts for the top 1 percent of households, which equals about 0.6 percent of GDP, is larger than the entire Social Security deficit, according to the CBO. Medicare is by far the bigger fiscal time bomb, and Bush's prescription drug plan made Medicare's looming shortfall far worse. Congress and the president doled out pork, special favors, corporate tax breaks, and other new spending at a pace that would be unsustainable in the short run and catastrophic over the long haul. The best way to strengthen Social

Security and Medicare is for Washington to stop spending the family fortune on everything else.

Corporations and individuals, meanwhile, don't have the option of such imprudence. They can't properly plan for the future because they're struggling to survive the here and now. Not so long ago, corporate America provided a reliable pillar of our long-term financial security: the pension. Like Social Security, the "defined-benefit plan" (corporations have not only often stopped offering pensions but have stopped calling them pensions) was initially designed to provide a great deal of security for a relatively short period of time. Now that retirees are living longer, and other costs like retiree health benefits are soaring, established corporations are straining under the weight of the existing defined-benefit plans, and few businesses are willing to take the risk of offering new ones.

According to the Center for Retirement Research at Boston College, the percentage of workers covered by a defined-benefit plan has been cut in half over the last quarter century. In 1980, 28 percent of workers depended on defined-benefit pensions, 8 percent depended on defined-contribution IRAs or 401(k)'s, and another 11 percent had both. The latest figures, from 2003, are the reverse: 5 percent with only a defined-benefit plan, 31 percent with only a 401(k) or IRA, and 14 percent with both.

Several embattled corporations, including Bethlehem Steel and United Airlines, have defaulted on their pension plans, and several more—such as GM—may yet do so.

Even financially sound, well-run, thriving companies are getting out of the pension business. This past year, IBM announced that it was suspending its defined-benefit plan and converting to defined contributions.

A pension is hard to beat, but defined-contribution plans done right have much to offer. Indeed, provided we maintain Social Security as a strong, solid, defined benefit plan, employees who are able to take full advantage of 401(k)-style plans at work can still enjoy a safe, secure retirement. But because defined-contribution plans are by nature more unpredictable, we need a new set of social arrangements that captures the potential of the 401(k) revolution and limits its downsides.

Individuals can't pick up the slack on their own. Last year, the nation had a negative savings rate because families are tapped out after four years without a raise. Only half of U.S. workers participate in employer-sponsored retirement plans, and 80 percent of small business employees have no retirement plan at all. According to the Retirement Security Project, seventy-one million Americans work for an employer that doesn't offer a retirement plan, and another seventeen million who could take part in an employer plan don't. More than half of all households have no retirement savings beyond Social Security. The median 401(k) balance for people between the ages of fifty-five and fifty-nine is only $15,000.

The mobility of today's workforce makes saving and planning for retirement more difficult as well. The average worker can expect to change jobs several times, which brings the promise of economic advancement but also the burden of navigating and managing half a dozen or more retirement plans. For most of us, the proliferation of choices—a seemingly endless supply of brokers, mutual funds, and financial instruments to choose from—is less a blessing than a curse, in two ways.

First, few people who manage their own money come out ahead as a result. Most index funds—which mirror major indexes like the Standard & Poor's 500 rather than trying to pick winning stocks—outperform expert money managers, let alone amateurs. Second, the sheer number of choices scares many people off altogether, or makes them unduly cautious. For most investors, simplicity trumps choice.

Unfortunately, the current hodgepodge of retirement plans fails to provide some of what American workers and businesses need most: flexibility and certainty. When only half the workforce is covered by private retirement plans, and the most generous of those plans are disappearing rapidly, the pension system looks more and more like a lottery. We expect too little, save too little, and provide too little for the long haul.

A 401(k) with Every Job

It doesn't have to be that way. The current system is more the result of inertia, not choice or expense. Millions of workers fail to sign up for the retirement plan their employer offers simply because they never get around to it or can't decide where to invest. Yet when employers that offer a 401(k) automatically enroll their employees (while allowing them to opt out), an overwhelming percentage of workers choose to stay in the system, and welcome the fact that a small portion of each paycheck is being set aside for their retirement. These defined-contribution plans are no trouble for employers, either. Many employers gladly choose to match a portion of their workers' payroll deductions. For employers that don't offer a match, the only burden is finding an investment firm to run the plan, and sending the payroll contributions its way.

As William Gale, Jonathan Gruber, and Peter Orszag of the Hamilton Project have suggested, a centerpiece of the new social contract must be a new private pension system based on the needs and responsibilities of twenty-first-century employees and employers. First, we should require all employers to offer workers a pension or 401(k), and expect all workers to contribute unless they make an affirmative step to opt out. To make life easier for workers, every employee would automatically be enrolled in the employer's 401(k), with the choice to opt out at any time. If employees switch jobs, they could take their account with them to a new employer. Employers could enroll each worker in their own plan, or in a state-sponsored retirement plan similar to the federal Thrift Savings Plan.

Automatic enrollment works. At R. R. Donnelly, a major

printing corporation based in Chicago, participation rates jumped from 68 percent to 92 percent within months of offering automatic enrollment.

As Gale, Gruber, and Orszag suggest, the "automatic 401(k)" ought to come with automatic escalation, automatic investment, and automatic rollover. In other words, companies should include an automatic "step-up" provision so that savings contributions increase as salaries increase. That way, workers' nest eggs can keep growing at the same pace as their ability to save. Savings should be invested directly in balanced, low-cost funds. When employees change jobs, they should be able to take their savings with them. Workers would have the freedom to change all these options, but for once, they would come out ahead if all they ever do is their jobs.

Tax reform can help. We need to consolidate the alphabet soup of retirement account provisions in the tax code into a single Universal Pension.

As our former White House colleague Gene Sperling, author of *The Pro-Growth Progressive,* has written, the current structure of savings incentives is upside down, providing the greatest subsidy to those who need it least.

In 2004, federal income tax refunds totaled nearly $230 billion. Over one hundred million taxpayers receive refunds averaging more than $2,000 each. As the IRS has finally recognized, we should give taxpayers the simple option of direct deposit—directing a portion of their refunds into retirement savings. Tax expert J. Mark Iwry calls it a "savable moment"—the one day we can turn America from a nation of consumers into a nation of savers literally overnight.

Finally, we should provide a new incentive to those hard-strapped Americans who currently can least afford to save. The Retirement Savings for Working Americans Act would make the Saver's Credit permanent and refundable, giving individuals earning up to $30,000 and couples up to $60,000 a 50 percent matching contribution for retirement savings of up to $2,000 a year. A recent study by H&R Block and the Retirement Security Project found that taxpayers who received a 50 percent match were nearly six times more likely to contribute (and contributed 50 percent more) than those who received no match.

Our current savings regime largely misses out on the cardinal rule of retirement planning: Start early and keep at it. Because of the miracle of compound interest, the amount a person contributes is not nearly as important as contributing it over a long period of time. Many Americans don't start saving until they think they can afford it, when they're our age or older. These proposals solve that problem by making saving virtually universal. Over the long haul, a little savings goes a very long way. If the employer matches her contribution, a person who starts setting aside 1 percent of her $30,000 salary at twenty-five and keeps doing it until she is sixty-five can expect to have a nest egg of around $200,000.

For employers and taxpayers, this whole plan costs next

to nothing. But for society as a whole, the benefits are enormous. Instead of a workforce where half have no retirement savings plan, an overwhelming majority of workers will have plans—and those who don't will have made that choice for themselves. Instead of thinking 401(k)'s are for lawyers, doctors, executives, and federal employees, every American will know there's a 401(k) in the future. And instead of a society with a negative savings rate that worries more about the minimum payment on monthly credit card bills than about providing for a secure retirement, America will once again be a place with an ethic of saving. Instead of defaulting on our future, providing for the future will be our default option.

Other Ways to Create Wealth

Enabling individuals to save more will do a great deal for Americans' economic security. But in the global economy, we must find ways to spread the circle of wealth and opportunity as well. Our country was founded on the principle that all men are created equal. For two centuries, the words of President Andrew Jackson have been an American mantra: "Equal opportunity for all, special privilege for none." Although we have yet to realize that goal, we aspire to be a classless society—a middle-class country in which the doors of opportunity are open to all.

Of late, our progress toward that ideal has stalled. The economic boom of the 1990s proved that incomes could go up across the board. But for much of the past three decades, and especially in this one, the wealth and ownership gaps in our society have widened. While most Americans have struggled not to lose ground, the upper and upper middle classes have hit the jackpot. Two economic trends are stacked in their favor: They are far more likely to have college degrees, in an economy that puts a premium on such credentials, and having higher incomes to start with means they are far more likely to be investors, in an economy that puts a premium on capital.

If we want to preserve the American Dream, we have to democratize those trends. Retirement saving is only one of many steps we should take to widen the circle of wealth.

Making Every Worker an Owner

First, we must overhaul the tax code to promote wealth for those who need it, not just those who already have it. As we explain later, we should make it easier for ordinary families to own homes, by allowing the deduction of mortgage interest by every homeowner, not just by those who itemize their taxes. We also must end the Republicans' war on work, which taxes a millionaire at a lower rate for his stock trades than it taxes the wages his secretary earns for placing the call to his broker. Eliminating the capital gains tax on the middle class—and restoring it for the wealthy—will help make sure America is a country where work leads to wealth, and where you don't have to be rich to get ahead.

We need to raise the minimum wage—and we need an economy that raises incomes across the board. Yet people who go to work every day should earn more than rising paychecks; those who make the economy grow deserve a stake in its growth. Some of our best companies recognize this and give their workers the chance to own stock in the enterprise they're helping to build. But at many American corporations, the division of capital is the same as in John D. Rockefeller's day: Workers get wages; only management gets to own a stake—at levels of executive compensation that would make Rockefeller blush.

In 1993, the Clinton administration tried to limit executive pay by eliminating the tax deductibility of salaries above $1 million. Executives responded by rewarding themselves with millions of dollars' worth of stock options instead. This time, we should approach the problem from the other direction and require companies that provide stock options to their executives to provide stock options to every worker. That way, no matter what executives do for themselves, workers will get a larger stake. Every worker should be an owner, not just the board of directors, a few VPs, and the CEO. If a secretary who helped start Microsoft can go on to be a millionaire, as has happened, every employee at other companies ought to have a stake in success.

Finally, we need to recognize that an Ownership Society won't work unless it comes with a warranty. As these proposals suggest, our future depends more than ever on the vitality of our markets—which is all the more reason we cannot leave financial markets to protect themselves. In the last few years, the national government has ceded that job to the states. State attorneys general like Eliot Spitzer of New York have been forced to police the mutual fund industry and a host of other complex financial institutions with little or no help from the feds. Watchdogs in Albany and Des Moines shouldn't have to protect the integrity of the global economy all by themselves. A vibrant American economy is possible only if the Securities and Exchange Commission and other federal regulators step up and take the lead. Strong national enforcement is actually probusiness, because corporations don't want fifty different sets of rules. Business leaders from the board room to Wall Street should welcome efforts to keep markets transparent; to make financial information easier to obtain, understand, and trust; and to defend the integrity of free enterprise by punishing all who put it at risk. Corporations should be held accountable for the promises they've made to their workers and should not be allowed to walk away from their pension plans and stick taxpayers with the tab.

Since its inception, America has sought to expand opportunity and democratize capitalism. Together, these measures—the universal 401(k), tax reform, options for all, and markets we can trust—will provide an aging society with universal retirement security, give the next generation a leg up, and help all Americans get ahead. A new social contract based on universal ownership and security will couple two potent forces: the unmatched dynamism of the American economy and Americans' unparalleled willingness, when given the chance, to work hard and build a better life for themselves and their children.

CHAPTER 8

HOUSE CALL: Universal Children's Health Care

If Americans wonder why their employer hasn't been able to give them a pay raise in the twenty-first century, it's not hard to find the culprit: Health insurance premiums got a big raise instead. Premiums are increasing at four times the rate of inflation and went up 73 percent after Bush took office. The average cost of a family policy is rising nearly $1,000 a year. At that blistering pace, employers are stuck: As long as health costs keep going up, incomes won't.

If you were looking to whip our $2.1-trillion annual health expenditure into shape, you certainly wouldn't start by hiring Republicans in Washington, who in 2004 ran a $413-billion deficit on a $2.3-trillion budget. That said, neither party is likely to be able to overhaul one-sixth of the U.S. economy—which is what health costs represent—without a little help from the other side.

The biggest barrier to universal coverage is what made coverage an issue to begin with: cost. Until something is done to rein in costs, none of the players who might be asked to help pay for universal coverage—not the government, not employers, not individuals—can even begin to afford it. A recent study in the journal *Health Affairs* found that the U.S. spends $5,267 per capita on health care—twice the median for the industrialized world, and $1,812 more than the nearest competitor, Switzerland. To put the U.S. on the road to universal coverage, we first have to tackle the cost spiral that has made that goal more and more elusive. We pay more for health care than any other nation on earth, and we don't get our money's worth.

In 1992, we helped the governor of a small southern state crisscross the country, waving a book called *Putting People First*. "The American health-care system costs too much and does not work," Bill Clinton and Al Gore wrote in June 1992. "It leaves 60 million Americans without adequate health insurance and bankrupts our families, our businesses, and our federal budget." They explained that since 1980, the average cost of health insurance had tripled to $3,000 a year, taking a severe economic and social toll: "Every year working men and women are forced to pay more while their employers cover less. Small businesses are caught between going broke and doing right by their employees." *Putting People First* spelled out the price America was paying for political inaction:

> Washington has ignored the needs of middle-class families and let health-care costs soar out of control.

> . . . Twelve years ago, Americans spent $249 billion on health care. This year we'll spend more than $800 billion. Health care costs are now the number one cause of bankruptcy and labor disputes. They threaten our ability to compete, adding, for example, $700 to the cost of every car made in America.

Fourteen years later, the only change in the health care story is numbers that are much, much worse. Instead of sixty million Americans without adequate health insurance, more than eighty million Americans go without insurance at some point during each year. Instead of $700, health care now adds $1,500 to the cost of every car GM makes in America. Instead of $249 billion in 1980 and $800 billion in 1992, we'll spend about $2.1 trillion in 2006. Instead of $3,000 a year, an average family health insurance policy costs around $11,000.

Washington has proved the Harry-and-Louise theory of cost containment: Do nothing about health care, and costs will triple every decade.

As battle-scarred veterans of the Clinton White House, we're not looking for a way to bring out all the defenders of the health care status quo just for old time's sake. Our goal is to suggest what America can get done, as quickly as possible, to keep businesses, working families, and the country from going bust.

The Sickly Politics of Health Care

American companies and their workers are already reeling from the health care burden—and unless something is done, their plight will only get worse. Together, the twin trend lines of increased global competition and an aging population threaten to bring our economy to a standstill. Our competitors started out paying far less for health care, and their advantage widens with each passing year. Health costs are now 16 percent of U.S. Gross Domestic Product, compared with 5 percent in 1960. The U.S. economy has been forced to perform like an aging runner in a global steeplechase. With each passing lap, our hurdles have grown higher and our breath shorter.

Employers have responded as any economic model would predict, shedding whatever costs they can to keep going. The share of businesses offering insurance to their employees went down from 69 percent to 60 percent between 2000 and 2005. Health care deductibles are rising 20 percent a year. Companies that did the right thing by their workers in the last century face a double whammy in this one: keeping their promises to pay pensions *and* the soaring health costs of retirees who are living longer.

The one major step Washington took on health care in the Bush years—the Medicare prescription drug bill—produced more bureaucracy and confusion than dependable benefits and cost containment. Its countless shortcomings were no accident because, as usual, the

Bush White House's motivation for enacting the bill was politics, not substance. Americans over sixty-five vote in higher proportions than those in any other age group. For the past decade, they have been the most hotly contested voter bloc, and prescription drug costs are their most pressing issue. Conservatives vehemently opposed the idea of creating an expensive new federal entitlement. But Karl Rove's plan for a permanent Republican realignment turned on buying seniors' gratitude—and he and Bush were willing to pay any price.

For years, political scientists will teach the prescription drug fiasco as a case study in how a bad bill becomes law. In their hearts, many congressional Republicans despised the bill as much as Democrats did. The administration's own experts at the Department of Health and Human Services knew the costs were understated. Senior citizens tried to warn that the bill would create more problems than solutions. The nation's pharmacists predicted it would be a bureaucratic nightmare. But every philosophical, practical, and fiscal objection was overruled in the name of politics. The White House wasn't interested in whether the bill worked anywhere except at the ballot box.

The drug bill is a perfect political morality tale, for that very reason. As the Bush administration learned the hard way, senior citizens had exactly the opposite goal as Karl Rove. They weren't looking for a political party to spend their golden years with. They weren't worrying about

Election Day; they were worrying about how to afford the drugs they have to take the entire year. Ironically, the White House failure on the only thing seniors cared about—the policy—undermined the only thing the White House cared about: the politics.

Republicans aren't alone in trying to score political points on health care. In the late 1990s, some congressional Democrats pleaded with the Clinton White House not to reach agreement on a Patients' Bill of Rights, for fear of losing an issue they wanted to use against Republicans in November. Unlike America, they were in luck: Republicans didn't want to reach agreement either. A few congressional elections later, what we had told those Democrats at the time proved true: The list of good ideas killed by congressional Republicans was by then so long, we could have passed a few items on our wish list and still left voters plenty of grievances against the other side for years to come.

In order to pass the prescription drug bill, Karl Rove promised his party that it was essential to ensuring their side's reelection. Every two years, Democratic consultants whisper the same message in their candidates' ears: This will finally be the year that Democratic candidates win the election on health care. It seems the only ones who can't be fooled into thinking they're winning on health care are all the American families and businesses stuck paying the bills.

Five Ways to Cut Costs

Every other major industry in America has gone through a revolution in innovation, productivity growth, and cost containment. Now it's health care's turn. If computers and superstores can save us money, so can doctors and CAT scans. We need a national crusade to bring America's health care system into the twenty-first century. Here are five commonsense ways to cut costs and improve quality through modernization and accountability.

First, we can make sure the productivity revolution that transformed much of the U.S. economy over the past decade finally finds its way into the health care system. Information technology has dramatic potential to reduce costs and improve patient outcomes. Many of the estimated ninety eight thousand annual deaths from medical errors could be prevented by better information and communication. Senator Hillary Clinton and former House Speaker Newt Gingrich have spoken out about the importance of electronic medical records. Health care will cost less when a doctor has immediate access to your full medical history, gives you an electronic prescription that doesn't depend on the pharmacist's deciphering her handwriting, and knows not to run duplicative tests. As Senator Clinton has pointed out, a country that wastes 34 cents on the dollar in administrative costs—15 cents more than any other nation—had better learn to use "21st century technology to eliminate 20th century bureaucracy." A RAND study last year estimated the potential health care savings from information technology at a staggering $162 billion a year.

Second, we need to structure the health care system to reward results. That means paying providers based on the quality of outcomes, not just the number of procedures. In other industries, the notion of paying fee-for-service is as outdated as the house call. The future of medicine should be fee-for-results.

Third, the health care system should help people stay healthy in the first place. No government program can work unless it asks personal responsibility in return. In our efforts to hold down costs and expand coverage, we should recognize how much a personal responsibility revolution in the health care system can do to advance both these goals. As we offer coverage, we ought to insist that individuals show up for free physicals to identify existing health problems and prevent future ones. Health providers and employers should be rewarded for steering recipients into serious fitness and wellness plans. Like car and home insurance, health insurance plans should reward responsible behavior.

Fourth, effective care is the most cost-effective care. Government is the largest purchaser of health care in America and ought to be leading the effort to figure out which treatments work best. We could save a fortune and improve outcomes by increasing research into the comparative effectiveness of everything from pharmaceuticals to the treatment of major diseases.

Fifth, we can save the most by doing a better job in the area where we spend the most: chronic care. Chronic care managers can achieve dramatic savings—and dramatically better results—by making sure their patients get the right care and take the right actions. Helping an emphysema patient to quit smoking or a heart patient to exercise is not only more cost-effective, but also better medicine.

Covering Every Child in America

As we put America on the road to achieving these savings, the goal of universal health care will no longer seem out of reach. But to get there, we have to learn from history. Four presidents have sought universal health care; four presidents have come up short. Yet, although our country remains a long way from universal coverage, it *has* done a great job of universalizing health care for seniors, veterans, and low-income families—segments of the population that wouldn't otherwise have it. To build on these successes, we propose three national goals that would make a significant down payment on the ultimate objective of ensuring affordable, meaningful, and accountable health care for every American: covering all children;

preparing the Medicare program for its demographic date with the Baby Boomers; and making employees' health coverage affordable for our nation's small businesses.

Despite Washington's intransigence, real progress is possible. One of the real social policy success stories of the past decade is unheralded: the State Children's Health Insurance Program (SCHIP) that President Clinton demanded as part of the 1997 Balanced Budget Act. When Clinton proposed the plan in his 1997 State of the Union, he said it would cover 5 million children. The program kept that promise, and it covered 5.8 million children in 2005.

The success of SCHIP is a bright spot in an otherwise grim litany of health care statistics. Over the past decade, the percentage of employers who provide health insurance to their workers has dropped steadily, and the ranks of the uninsured have grown by six million since 2000. But thanks to Medicaid and SCHIP, the percentage of uninsured children has actually declined.

Our next mission must be to finish the job that Medicaid and the SCHIP have done so much to advance: ensuring health care for every child in America. In Illinois, Governor Rod Blagojevich has already done that through a program called All Kids, which makes comprehensive health insurance available to every child in the state at rates the child's parents can afford. Massachusetts, with its new individual mandate to require all citizens to purchase health care, is doing the same. When Congress renews the SCHIP in 2007, we should reach across party lines to agree on universal health care for children. As a nation we should require every parent in American to obtain health insurance for her or his children, and we should provide the support they need to afford it.

A National Cure Center

Second, we must prepare our health care system for the burdens of an aging society. The greatest fiscal challenge of the twenty-first century isn't Social Security, or national defense, or even George Bush's reckless tax cuts and wanton spending. It is the Medicare and Medicaid costs of the Baby Boom generation's becoming the Senior Boom. Medicare's trustees now say the system will go broke in 2018—just twelve years away, and twelve years earlier than their projection when Bush took office. As the Medicare population doubles from forty million to more than eighty million people, new ways to finance and more efficiently deliver necessary care will become not just desirable but absolutely essential. And although we will never have anywhere near the resources if we continue the fiscal madness of the Bush administration, we cannot pretend that the health care cost challenges will go away without an aggressive effort to modernize these programs as well.

We must confess that we don't have a plan to secure Medicare solvency through the latter half of the twenty-first century, but we can begin now to start saving the Medicare trust fund money. The Medicare Payment Advisory Commission, an independent federal body created by the Balanced Budget Act of 1997, has recommended a series of sensible payment reforms that together would save $60 billion a year. The Bush administration was irresponsible to create a gobsmackingly expensive new drug entitlement, conceal its cost, and then rule out trying to get the best drug prices. Early in 2006, fifty-four senators—including eleven Republicans—defied the president by voting to give Medicare the authority to compete with private plans to negotiate the best price for prescription drugs. In addition, we can achieve more savings, better efficiency, and improved care if we more aggressively pursue and implement chronic care management programs within the Medicaid and Medicare programs. Since two-thirds of Medicare spending is on patients with five or more chronic conditions, we would be foolish not to spend much more time focusing on these populations and creating incentives for states to do the same in their Medicaid programs. The potential savings from all these steps would go a long way toward extending the life of the Medicare trust funds—and the prescription drug program.

And precisely because our society is getting older, we need to not only improve our ability to manage chronic illnesses but also seek cures for them. As we spend hundreds of billions treating diseases like cancer, diabetes, and

Alzheimer's, imagine what we could save by curing them. Instead of standing in the way of stem cell research, Washington should let science, not politics, drive the search for cures. We also favor an idea that already has broad bipartisan support: a National Cure Center dedicated to finding cures for chronic diseases. The premier public engine of medical advances, the National Institutes of Health, has a broad mission for basic medical research. A National Cure Center would marshal the talents of research scientists inside government and out in a public-private effort to set clear milestones in the search for cures. This idea would remedy a market failure: Private research efforts by pharmaceutical companies and device manufacturers largely focus on treating chronic diseases, not curing them outright or preventing them in the first place. Drug makers are slow to produce vaccines, for example, because they can't recoup their investment from patients who need only one dose. Likewise, our relatively modest public investment in cures discounts the enormous savings from actually curing chronic disease. Polio once cost a great deal to treat. Thanks to a vaccine, the disease no longer exists in the United States. Alzheimer's costs us an estimated $100 billion a year; a cure would empty half the nursing-home beds in America. Without scientific discoveries that actually cure people, not just prolong their treatment, we will be hard-pressed to afford the retirement of the Baby Boom generation.

Every American Ought to Get the Same Health Care As Congress

If there's one economic sector that needs help more than any other, it's our small businesses, the backbone of the American economy. A third of Americans work at a business with fewer than a hundred employees, and small business creates most of the new jobs in our economy. Moreover, small business entrepreneurship is one of our greatest comparative assets in the competition ahead. Many of the Fortune 500 companies—including powerhouses like Home Depot and Google—didn't even exist thirty years ago.

Although large companies like General Motors get the most attention in the health care debate because they carry the twin burden of vast retiree populations and generous benefit plans, the high cost of health care is just as troublesome for small businesses and their employees. Most of the forty-six million uninsured in America are working people, and the vast majority of uninsured workers work for small businesses. Only about half of small businesses provide health insurance for their employees because it is so difficult to find policies they or their workers can afford. In any insurance market, price and risk depend on the size of the pool. Large pools like Medicare or the Federal Employees Health Benefits Program (FEHBP) can contain costs because they spread the risk across a huge population. Small businesses suffer the opposite fate: The smaller the pool, the worse the deal.

Instead of leaving small businesses to fend for themselves, we should give them the opportunity to pool their purchasing power. The best purchasing pool in the country, not surprisingly, is the one that covers members of Congress: the FEHBP. With a pool of eight million people, this program lets federal workers choose from up to two hundred different health plans, empowering them to demand quality health coverage for an affordable price.

Every American ought to have access to the same health coverage that members of Congress enjoy. Senators Richard Durbin and Blanche Lincoln and Representative Ron Kind have introduced a plan to do just that. The Small Employers Health Benefits Program Act would create an FEHBP-like plan with the benefits of group purchasing power, lower administrative costs, and greater choice. Any business with up to one hundred employees could participate. The Durbin bill provides employers a substantial tax credit to help reimburse their health care expenses. As in the federal program, individuals would get a choice of health plans. While the Durbin bill creates a nationwide program, the federal government could work with states to create statewide programs as well.

If we could start from scratch, we wouldn't design an employer-based health care system, which is left over from the World War II, when government-imposed wage controls forced employers to find another way to attract workers.

For the long haul, one of the most promising health ideas we've heard comes from our family physician: Dr. Ezekiel Emanuel, the eldest of the Emanuel brothers, who made his parents proud by becoming a doctor, not a congressman. In *Boston Review,* Zeke and Dr. Victor Fuchs eloquently explain the challenge:

> For both religious and economic reasons, individualism has always been at the center of American political values. And America's conception of equality is rooted in this individualism: the United States is a land of opportunity, not economic security; our commitment is to equality of opportunity, not equality of outcome. As a consequence, compared with Canada and most of Western Europe, we have a smaller government with much less responsibility for social and economic problems, leaving more for individuals to pursue in the private market.

Emanuel and Fuchs remind us that those who long for a single-payer system or the sweeping safety nets of other nations should not forget why presidents as diverse as Harry Truman and Richard Nixon couldn't enact them: "We should not confuse what we desire and think would be best for the country with what is consonant with deeply ingrained values." In the *New England Journal of Medicine,* Emanuel and Fuchs proposed an approach consistent with those values: "a voucher system for universal health care," which would provide every American under sixty-five a voucher for basic health services from the insurance company or health plan of his or her choice. Universal vouchers attempt to merge the most appealing elements from across the political spectrum. Everybody would be covered with a meaningful, clinically based benefit, as Democrats argue; all would choose where they get their coverage, as Republicans insist; covering basic rather than comprehensive services would keep from breaking the bank, as taxpayers demand.

Emanuel and Fuchs are the first to admit that their plan is well beyond Washington's current reach. We're not eager to abandon the employer system when past reforms have come up short and the Republicans seem determined to leave a far less reliable alternative in its place. But as we succeed in bringing America's health costs under control and putting the country on the road to universal coverage, we should keep the Emanuel-Fuchs principle in mind for the long term.

Nothing in health care is ever easy. The advantage of the ideas in this chapter—universal children's health care, a productivity revolution to cut costs and improve quality, new cures for an aging society, affordable coverage for small business—is that they can actually happen. Over the years, no issue has stymied the political system more than health care. Our economic system now depends on making real progress.

CHAPTER 9

THE ERA OF HACK GOVERNMENT IS OVER: Fiscal Responsibility and An End to Corporate Welfare

For America to have a new social contract, Washington needs to hold up its end of the bargain. From widespread corporate welfare to Hack-ridden bureaucracy, we must end the political abuses that have given us the worst government money can buy. We need a president and a Congress willing to spend more on the future and less on the past. When America's way of life is threatened by terror from one direction and economic competition from another, we cannot fight and win one war without fighting and winning the other. One of George Bush's great failures in the war on terror was never recognizing how much economic burdens at home can add to our burdens abroad. Instead of planning for a long two-front war to defeat terror and to remain the economic superpower, Republican tax and spending policies drained the nation's war chest and made it difficult for us to afford either goal.

No American president before Bush had cut taxes in wartime, with good reason: Wars are expensive. During

World War II, FDR raised the rate on the top tax bracket to 94 percent—not because he hated the rich, or because supply-side economics hadn't been invented yet, but because he wanted the U.S. to be able to fight for as long as it took to win. Republicans were justifiably proud that the Reagan defense buildup helped spend the Soviets into submission. This time, Republicans tried their best to do the same to America.

According to Gene Sperling, "Bush fiscal policy is the single largest factor in the worst fiscal deterioration in history—eventually worsening our fiscal position by $400–500 billion a year." The Bush deficits were by political design. Compassionate conservatism was a politically clever and patently misleading way to promise conservatives that he would cut taxes—and promise the rest of the country that he wouldn't cut government to pay for it.

No president since Thomas Jefferson went so long without a single veto either. When the president wouldn't say no, neither would his own party in Congress. Republicans' message to the voters seemed to be "Stop us before we spend again."

Cut and Invest

In World War II, FDR took drastic measures not simply to finance the war, but to show the country that our soldiers shouldn't be the only ones to sacrifice. Today, Washington needs to tighten its belt not just to keep our Chinese creditors at bay, but to show that responsibility begins at the top. As then Senator John Edwards once said in a speech to the Democratic Leadership Council, "Mr. President, if you're not going to use that word responsibility, could we please have it back?"

The only sensible strategy to put the nation's fiscal house in order is what economist Rob Shapiro dubbed "cut and invest." Believe it or not, it isn't that hard to find ways to trim the bloated federal budget. Paul Weinstein of the Progressive Policy Institute has identified a list of $1.8 trillion in potential savings over the next ten years. There are three levers to get the deficit back under control: Get rid of programs and privileges we don't need anymore; close loopholes that let some distort the market; and put the economy back on a path of sustained, broad-based economic growth.

First, a society that ended welfare for single mothers had better be willing to end welfare for corporations. Corporate welfare warps the values of our economic policy every bit as much as the old welfare system warped the values of our social policy. If we believe in free enterprise, competition, and free markets, we must pledge to end corporate welfare as we know it. Nothing would do more to prove that the national government is leaving behind the old politics of corruption in order to prepare America for the new economic competition. We favor a binding commission, long championed by Senators John McCain and

Joe Lieberman, to cut corporate welfare. When Congress needed to find the nerve to modernize our defense commitments at the end of the Cold War, it created the Base Realignment and Closure Commission (BRAC), which spares members from having to vote for particular base closings by recommending a comprehensive package for a single up-or-down vote. A bipartisan base-closing-style corporate welfare commission would force members who want to defend outrageous spending to cast an outrageous public vote. Independent estimates suggest that cuts in corporate welfare could easily save at least $200 billion over ten years.

Next, we need new rules to fundamentally change the way Washington sets priorities. To begin with, we need to restore two bipartisan, commonsense principles that helped us produce budget surpluses the last time: annual spending caps and a pay-as-you-go rule that Congress can't pass new programs or tax cuts without a means to pay for them. In the past, those rules proved remarkably effective because they gave everyone a shared stake in fiscal discipline. Appropriators knew that winking at a colleague's boondoggle meant less room for their own priorities. Tax writers had an easy rejoinder to special pleading for a tax cut: Tell us what you'd cut to pay for it. The Bush administration abandoned those rules to make way for all the tax cuts and supplemental appropriations it couldn't pay for. With no means to enforce discipline, Congress and the administration were like dieters refusing to exercise or count calories—and it didn't take long for the budget to get fat and stay that way.

A Future Budget

To meet the challenges we have outlined in this book, another new paradigm is needed. For many years, Felix Rohatyn, a leading economic thinker and financier on Wall Street, has called on the federal government to follow the lead of most states and develop a separate capital budget for long-term investments. He calls it "a trust fund for America." In the early 1990s, economist Rob Shapiro proposed a similar idea: a "future budget" that would be separate from the annual consumption budget. The principle behind these ideas makes perfect sense: Some government spending is a genuine investment that will more than pay for itself over time by making the country more productive and efficient. Other government spending is designed solely for the moment—to repair past mistakes, alleviate current pressures, or, in many cases, to serve immediate political needs by spending or giving money away. Far too often, the narrow political urgency of the moment crowds out the nation's best interests for the long term.

The purpose of a future budget is to give America's long-term interests a fighting chance in Washington. A clearly defined, tightly targeted future budget would leave room for smart investments that could pay for themselves over the long haul. So long as future needs were taken care of in a future budget, Democrats and Republicans might accept a strict requirement to balance the consumption side of the ledger.

Given Washington's fondness for loopholes, the rules for consideration in a future budget would have to be carefully drawn. Shapiro proposed a neutral, bipartisan board to distinguish investment from consumption. For example, medical research, federal support for R&D, and education would be considered investments; administrative costs and food stamp benefits would be consumption. Capital expenditures that increase productivity—for example, broadband—would be investments; the infamous "Bridge to Nowhere" earmark for an Alaskan boondoggle in the 2005 budget bill would be consumption.

Ending the Incumbent Protection Racket

At the same time, we need to restore accountability in politics by restoring competition. Twelve years ago, Republicans won the House and Senate on a promise of congressional, ethical, and lobbying reform. Now they couldn't care less about living up to the Contract with America, even though Americans have it in writing.

Why? Because as Ed Kilgore of the Democratic Leadership Council has written, for most the fix is in: The House member always wins. Across the country, congressional redistricting has become an engine of polarization, partisanship, and incumbency. At a time when the electorate is almost evenly divided, only one in eight congressional races ends up closer than 10 points. In our democracy, it has come to this: Members are far more likely to leave Congress to become lobbyists than to be defeated for reelection.

In some states, like Texas, ruthless gerrymandering has been used for partisan gain. Georgia's recent congressional redistricting plan was overturned because it required voters without drivers' licenses to purchase an identification card—a throwback to the poll tax of the Jim Crow era. In other states, the two parties have linked arms to protect every incumbent from a competitive race. Voters used to get to pick their politicians; now politicians get to pick their voters. It's time to end the incumbent protection racket. Representative John Tanner has introduced a bill to require every state to appoint a bipartisan panel that would draw compact, contiguous districts without regard to the impact on incumbents. A gerrymandered political map cannot be a refuge from a failed agenda.

Monopolies are as harmful in politics as in the marketplace. Competition keeps incumbents honest. When politicians don't have to answer to the public, too often they learn to serve other masters. It's no accident that members of Congress caught up in scandal—such as Randy "Duke" Cunningham, Bob Ney, Tom DeLay, and Bill Jefferson—almost always come from safe districts where they know they'll never face real scrutiny of their actions. If we want true political reform, we need to bring competition to the system and make politicians answer to the voters for a change.

The Cost of One-Party Rule

Voters expect everyone in Washington to do their part. In the 1990s, we reduced the federal bureaucracy by nearly 400,000, but under this administration, bureaucracy is in bloom again. It's time to reduce the number of federal consultants by 100,000 and cut 10 percent of the federal civilian workforce that isn't involved in defense or homeland security. As Governor Tom Vilsack and others have suggested, members of Congress should pledge not to take another pay raise until the federal budget is back in balance and ordinary Americans' incomes are once again going up. All the special-interest lobbyists who want special favors from government should put their hands back in their pockets as Washington declares that the window is closed. Congress should not only do away with earmarks that direct spending to special projects in members' own districts but give the president the authority to rescind wasteful line items in the budget and send them back to Congress for an up-or-down vote—a line-item veto that would pass constitutional muster.

Finally, America faces enormous long-term budgetary challenges that will require a mammoth shift in the political culture away from special interest and special privilege to common interest and common purpose. We'll never find room for new ideas in the federal budget if we don't get rid of the old politics and petty corruption that have run us so deep into debt.

In recent years, the Republican majority reverted to what *Slate* editor Jacob Weisberg calls "interest-group conservatism." Every tax bill became a Christmas tree of expensive, narrow-interest baubles. Spending bills groaned under the weight of so many lobby-driven earmarks. A party already beholden to moneyed interests was unable to resist the temptation to govern by quid pro quo. The costs of this corruption spread so far that it was hard to tell where the ethics ended and the spending began. Sometimes the transactions were for private benefit. Duke Cunningham was sentenced to eight years for taking bribes. Often the transactions were partisan. Former House Majority Leader Tom DeLay and Senate Republican Conference Chair Rick Santorum met regularly with lobbyists to make sure they were advancing one another's interests.

Republicans cynically and deliberately aligned themselves with private interests. They coerced firms to hire Republican lobbyists and made businesses agree to support all the president's budget-busting tax cuts if they ever wanted to see another tax break. George Bush pledged to restore integrity to government, but instead his party restored payola and patronage to a degree not seen in generations. Accidentally, and much to his chagrin, DeLay may for once have done the country a service, by confirming what voters have long suspected: There's something rotten in Washington. From the Crédit Mobilier scandal of the 1870s, when congressmen gave the railroads government subsidies in exchange for stock, to Watergate in the 1970s, corruption has provided some of democracy's greatest teaching moments. Washington has never been entirely on the level. But of late, an unfortunate series of events—the polarization of American politics, the explosive growth of the lobbying industry, and the prolonged reign of one-party government—combined to give private interests their strongest grip on the nation's capital since the Gilded Age. The rules of the road weren't designed to withstand one-party rule. Without sweeping changes in the way Washington works, the interests of ordinary people don't stand a chance.

In part, the reason is that Bush did not keep his promise to "change the tone in Washington," or at least not in the way he said he would. As a result, the changes this company town needs are now much more profound. The bipartisanship of a Howard Baker, a lifelong Republican whose hard questions at the Watergate hearings helped bring down the Nixon administration, gave way to a partisan era crowded with people who spouted the party line first and asked questions later (or not at all). Trust is low, and the stakes are high—with a $2-trillion tax code up for grabs and a burgeoning influence industry competing for advantage.

As if controlling all three branches of government weren't enough, Republicans created another one with equal power: K Street. In today's Washington, the Fourth Estate is no longer the press; it's the lobbyists. The Founders imagined that three branches would provide checks and balances. The new fourth branch is more efficient: It just provides checks.

The Revolving Swamp

For more than a decade, Tom DeLay marshaled the K Street Project to muscle lobbying firms, trade associations, and companies into hiring only Republicans. DeLay helped turn K Street into Congress's back office: writing campaign checks and legislation, guaranteeing lifetime employment, making travel arrangements, providing caddies and sporting equipment.

There's nothing inherently wrong with lobbying. In a representative democracy, companies, groups, and individuals have the right to hire someone to represent their interests. All lobbyists maintain that they provide a service by helping government make informed decisions, and sometimes this is actually true. But let's face it: The laws lobbyists live by were written before the latest gold rush. According to Jeffrey Birnbaum of the *Washington Post,* the number of registered lobbyists doubled in the last five years, as did the top fee lobbying firms charge their new clients.

Jack Abramoff, DeLay's favorite lobbyist, is the poster child for why the old rules don't work in the new moneyed era. The parable is one any conservative economist or preacher could have written: The wages of sin may be death, but you can't beat the year-end bonus.

We need to reform the political system so that Washington lives by a clear set of rules that protect the public interest. The place to start is by closing the revolving door. According to the Center for Public Integrity, more than 240 former members of Congress and agency heads are active lobbyists—double the number of a decade ago.

Something's wrong when the K Street Caucus of members-turned-lobbyists rivals the size of either party's caucus in the House of Representatives. If Washington were serious about reform, it would stop the revolving door for good and impose a five-year lobbying ban on members of Congress, their senior staff, and senior administration officials.

Lobbying shouldn't be a jobs program. In 1993, House Speaker Tom Foley warned Clinton not to pursue campaign finance and lobbying reform: "Members will think you're out to take away their current livelihoods and their future livelihoods in one fell swoop." The irony is painful, and instructive: Failing to embrace reform before the 1994 election was one reason Foley and a record number of his colleagues found themselves looking for that next job when it was over.

At the same time, we need to stop the money chase that takes public officials away from the job they're supposed to do. In the last presidential campaign cycle, each side spent more than a billion dollars. Members of Congress and lobbyists squander much of their waking lives on the Washington fund-raising circuit—and most of them hate it for taking them away from the job they're supposed to do for the American people. We should raise the level of political debate by making free advertising time for federal candidates available on the airwaves and the Internet, so Americans can make an informed choice.

Whacking the Hacks

If we want to take a whack out of government, we need to take the Hack out of government. In our experience, career federal employees don't rush to squander government's money—political Hacks do. Richard Foster, that career actuary who was almost fired from the Department of Health and Human Services, wasn't the one trying to conceal that Bush's Medicare plan would cost hundreds of billions of dollars more than the administration had told Congress; a Bush political appointee was.

The Congressional Budget Office doesn't estimate the savings from getting rid of big-spending political Hacks, but clearly, they would be considerable. Today, the federal workforce includes about three thousand political appointees. Cutting that number in half would save nearly $2 billion in personnel costs over ten years—and more important, it would reduce the ranks of officials who can order increased spending for political gain. Over time, it would pay another dividend, by reducing the pool of ex-officials who can lobby their former colleagues for special favors. Most important, cutting the number of Hacks in half would reduce the number of incompetents and ideologues in a position to do the country lasting, costly damage.

It's sad and ironic to take a stand for democracy in the Middle East at the same time it's taking such a beating in the Mid-Atlantic. But it's not too late for this sorry episode to have a happy ending. Some of the greatest strides in the history of the progressive movement—at the turn of the century and in the 1930s—were fueled by popular outrage at private intrigue on the public square. If we have the courage to embrace reform, even when it hurts, we'll do more than prosecute these scandals. We'll drain the swamp that breeds them.

And we can even make the economy stronger and the government more efficient, by cleaning up the place where the most politics is played and the most money is wasted: the tax code.

CHAPTER 10

THE IDES OF APRIL: Tax Reform to Help Those Who Aren't Wealthy to Build Wealth

Didn't we already give them a break at the top?
President Bush in 2002 to his advisers,
before proposing more tax breaks
for the wealthy anyway

It is time to put the tax code back in line with our values. If we're going to renew the social contract for an increasingly competitive world, our tax system should give Americans more opportunity and security, not more of the burden. We need tax reform that puts a cap on middle-class taxes, gives people who don't start out wealthy the chance to build wealth, and helps every American secure the pillars of middle-class life: raising a family, buying a home, paying for college, and saving for retirement.

For much of the past thirty years, the economic debate in Washington has revolved around one word: *taxes*. Now, there's nothing wrong with a healthy debate about taxes. For as long as humans have had armies and governments, we've argued over how best (and how much) to pay for them. The American Revolution broke out in part because our forefathers bitterly resented the British crown's Stamp Tax.

For much of American history, however, taxation has been at the fringes of the economic debate, not the core of it. To be sure, every new tax, tax shift, or tax increase has sparked prophecies of economic ruin. Theodore Roosevelt campaigned for graduated income and inheritance taxes—but would be run out of the Republican Party if he took that stand today.

What's most remarkable about how much taxes have dominated the economic debate for the past three decades is that the economy isn't the reason we've kept debating them. If the tax debate were really a debate about economic growth, it would change as the economy changed. Yet the tax debate in Washington never changes. In 1980, when the nation was battling sky-high inflation and interest rates, Republicans proposed lower taxes for the wealthy. In 1996 and 2000, when the economy was riding high and had just produced more millionaires than at any period in history, the Republican answer was lower taxes for the wealthy. In 2004, when the wealthy were still doing well, but ordinary families had taken a pay cut over the past four years, the GOP proposed cutting taxes for the wealthy.

Whenever economic circumstances changed in his first term, President Bush likewise changed the rationale for his tax cuts, but he never changed the policy. In 2000, when the economy was booming, Bush proposed tax cuts to get rid of the budget surplus and—unfortunately for the nation—succeeded beyond his wildest dreams. A year later, with the economy in recession, he promised the same tax cuts as stimulus. After the 9/11 attacks made clear that for years to come, the U.S. would be spending a fortune to fight the war on terror, Bush proposed more tax cuts as a return to normality. In 2003, as he headed for war in Iraq and a record deficit at home, he proposed still another round of tax cuts to ease the burden of wealth on the wealthy.

When Republicans talk about taxes, any resemblance to the actual economy is coincidental and unintentional. That's because the Republican case for tax cuts is a theological argument, not an economic one. Conservatives have to make taxes a theological debate because the supply-side theory is the economic equivalent of intelligent design: They don't have any evidence to teach it in the classroom. Perhaps the conservative movement's greatest political coup over the last quarter century was to pull off the notion that cutting taxes for the wealthy corresponds to any economic theory at all.

Feeding the Beast

Too often in recent years, Democrats inadvertently aided the conservative cause by making the supply-side argument in reverse, by suggesting that rolling back the Bush tax cuts is in and of itself a plan for economic growth. Keeping tax cuts for the wealthy from becoming permanent is an excellent idea because restoring fiscal discipline is a prerequisite for the nation's long-term economic health. But fiscal discipline is about much more than restoring progressivity to the tax code, and economic growth is about much more than fiscal discipline. When Democrats leave the impression that the economy will take off if we can just roll back the Republican tax cuts, our argument is closer to the truth than the Republicans', but a far cry from a full and effective economic theory.

Along the way, the Bush administration wiped out the one argument for tax cuts that bore the slightest relation to the economy, that they would help limit the size of government. If tax cuts actually led to smaller government, Republicans might be able to make that case. But supply-side Republicans have never been serious about limiting government. The Laffer Curve promising higher tax revenues from lower tax rates, which University of Southern California economist Arthur Laffer famously drew on the back of a napkin to sell conservatives on tax cuts, was designed to duck any tough choices. Notwithstanding conservative rhetoric, Reagan never pressed Congress to limit spending, and neither did Bush. In fact, Bush reached the White House by promising not to be antigovernment—one promise, at least, that he kept with abandon. Now Republicans don't even bother to argue for less government, except when it comes to investments in the future.

Instead, they've systematically increased current government spending and cut taxes at the same time. As a result, they're not really cutting taxes, just deferring them—borrowing money that we'll have to pay later, with interest, so they can attempt to buy votes now. The Republicans now promise more government—and they want to pay for it with more debt.

So for all the smoke and mirrors about economic growth, the tax debate is really a debate about values. Republicans want a tax code that puts the whole burden on work instead of wealth. Democrats want a progressive tax code that rewards work and asks the most of those who have been blessed with the most—and who have a great deal to gain from a more prosperous society.

The Republican War on Work

Of course, with one party in power in Washington, the tax debate wasn't much of a debate. Whenever Democrats worked up the courage to ask why this president was the first to cut taxes in wartime, Republicans accused us of waging class warfare. All we did was raise in public the concerns Bush raised to his advisers in private in 2002. If Bush once had qualms about giving more money to rich people, he seemed to get over it. As billionaire Warren Buffett has said, "If class warfare is being waged in America, my class is clearly winning." In Bush's class war, the middle class lost.

Although the supply-side theory failed badly enough in the Reagan era, it has turned out to be the worst possible failed theory for the era of globalization. Tax cuts increased the return on capital instead of the return on work—at the very moment the global marketplace did the same.

Payroll taxes make up the bulk of taxes paid by middle-class and poor Americans. Corporate taxes, which accounted for 30 percent of federal revenue fifty years ago, now provide just 10 percent. The Bush administration piled on the disparity by cutting every imaginable tax on wealth and shifting the burden onto those who work.

The heart of the middle class hasn't seen a pay raise in years, yet it is inheriting a greater share of the tax burden. The professional class—doctors, lawyers, CEOs—saw its taxes fall as its incomes rose and its wealth went up even faster. For all Bush's talk about the investor class, his cuts in the dividend and capital gains rates were meant to benefit a narrow sliver of the country. A *New York Times* study found that in 2003, the investment tax cuts saved 175,000 millionaires—about one-tenth of 1 percent of taxpayers—an average of $41,400 apiece. Households earning less than $50,000 saved an average of $10 apiece. That's Republicans' idea of progressivity: Millionaires with twenty times the income reaped four thousand times the gain.

Even if it weren't worsening a wealth and income gap that was getting worse to begin with, the Republican war on work would be a moral affront to America's values. As

Buffett has pointed out, something is wrong when a billionaire churning his stocks can pay a lower tax rate than his secretary. America is a land of workers, not heirs and heiresses. The idea that anyone should be able to rise as far as her determination and God-given talents can take her is the moral foundation of our economy and our society. The tragedy of the past few years is that while the global economy had already begun to make many Americans lose faith in that promise, their president did everything in his power to drive a stake through it.

As if favoring wealth over work weren't enough to put government out of line with America's values, the Bush administration and the Republicans in Congress put every aspect of the tax code up for auction. The last several years were a gold rush for lobbyists in Washington—with the most lucrative veins on the tax-writing committees in Congress. The return on lobbying is growing even faster than the return on wealth. In 2004, Congress had to pass a tax bill to fix a $5-billion-a-year compliance issue with the World Trade Organization. By the time Republicans were finished, the bill cost the taxpayers $137 billion over five years—and the WTO concluded that we still have a compliance problem.

American companies spend time and money chasing special tax breaks that distort the market, pad their stock prices, and shelter the companies from healthy competition. Lawmakers spend time—and take campaign money—in a cozy scheme to coddle contributors, when they ought to be making the tax code work for ordinary people. That's one great irony among the many of the Bush era: The tax code no longer even attempts to promote economic growth; it simply favors those with influence—which results in hindering growth.

Code Red

Those with wealth and those with lobbyists get special tax breaks. What do the American people get? A tax code that is complicated, burdensome, and completely at odds with their values. Consider: The tax code is now 1.4 million words long and spans ten thousand sections. Another ten thousand pages were added in the last year alone. It takes the average taxpayer thirty-three hours to complete the tax-filing process. More than half of filers use paid tax preparers. A stunning 70 percent of those who file for the Earned Income Tax Credit have to hire tax preparers. Every year, tax compliance costs the U.S. treasury about $115 billion. Meanwhile, the code is so riddled with loopholes that the IRS says approximately $345 billion a year in taxes goes uncollected because of tax avoidance and underpayments. That tax gap alone would be nearly enough to balance the federal budget.

With Republicans' help, special interests won subsidies, shelters, and loopholes, while middle-class families bore the brunt of a crushing tax burden and arcane IRS forms. In the twenty years since the last major tax reform, the tax code has gone Washington, with enough loopholes, shelters, and phaseouts to keep the influence industry booming. As a result, the current system rewards bad behavior, like tax avoidance, and punishes people who go to work every day and do the right thing.

The Washington swamp feeds off one source above all others: loopholes in the tax code. There's even a loophole for time spent writing loopholes. Legal expenses are tax-deductible; lobbying costs are not—all the more reason to hire that K Street hybrid, the lawyer-lobbyist. By underreporting lobbying expenditures and billing their hours as legal work instead, firms can save clients money—or charge them more. Take away the font of special privilege, and the culture around it will be hard-pressed to survive.

Our blueprint starts with the Wyden-Emanuel tax reform plan, sponsored by Rahm and Senator Ron Wyden of Oregon. That plan cuts the number of tax brackets in half, from six to three; closes dozens of loopholes by setting a corporate flat tax of 35 percent; does away with the Bush penalty on work; eliminates the Alternative Minimum Tax; and reduces the federal deficit by $100 billion over five years by cutting corporate welfare.

Under our plan, taxpayers will have to complete only a simple, one-page 1040. We want Americans to spend April at Little League games, at their place of worship, or in the great outdoors, not wasting thirty-three hours filling out tax forms.

Our proposal includes four "superincentives"—based on the work of Paul Weinstein at the Progressive Policy Institute—to help the middle class deal with the following challenges of the twenty-first-century economy.

College

A College Tax Credit will replace the five major existing education tax incentives—the Hope Scholarship, the Lifetime Learning Credit, the deduction for higher education expenses, the exclusion of employee provided education benefits, and the exclusion for qualified tuition reductions—with a simple $3,000-a-year credit. This credit will be fully refundable and available for four years of college and two years of graduate school. It will help six million full-time students, cover more than half the average cost of tuition at a public university, and help us toward our twenty-first-century goal of sending every American to college.

Home

A Universal Mortgage Deduction will give all homeowners a break, not just those who itemize. Today, only 28 percent of taxpayers and just half of homeowners itemize their deductions. As Paul Weinstein observes, only one-fifth of households with incomes below $50,000 receive the home-ownership deduction. That disparity contributes to another one: In a nation with a record number of homeowners, minority homeownership rates lag as much as 20 percent behind. By allowing nonitemizers to claim the mortgage interest deduction, our plan would both increase home-ownership and reduce the number of households that must file the more complicated 1040 tax form. If we're going to subsidize people with two or three homes, we should at least help young couples trying to own one.

Family

A Simplified Family Credit will reward work and discourage dependency by collapsing the Earned Income Tax Credit (EITC), the Child Credit, and the Dependent Credit into one credit for working families with children—while providing more benefits to more families than all of them combined. At the same time, it will eliminate two hundred pages of the tax code—red tape that falls hardest on people who need help the most. At clinics in Chicago, Rahm's Tax Assistance Program brings in expert volunteers to help families wrestle with instructions like "Enter the total of any net income from passive activities (included on Schedule E, lines 26, 29a (col. (g)), 34a (col. (d)), and 40. (See instructions below for lines 11 and 12.)" Right now, the IRS gives families a fifty-four-page

EITC instruction booklet for what ought to be a few lines on a 1040 form. Instead, they'll get a one-page form. Our goal is to reward work, not persistence in wading through bureaucracy. The IRS does just the opposite. According to IRS Taxpayer Advocate Nina Olson, at least 75 percent of the 1.6 million requests for tax refunds that were tagged as fraudulent and frozen over the past five years were from EITC applicants, the vast majority of whom had done nothing wrong. In our view, Americans who are working full time to try to join the middle class should be treated as heroes, not cheats.

Retirement

A Universal Pension will replace the current hodgepodge of sixteen existing IRA-type accounts with a single portable retirement account for all workers. This account would supplement existing 401(k)s from employers and help create an ethic of saving by strengthening incentives for middle-class workers. Over the past thirty years, Congress has created sixteen separate savings provisions—roughly one per Congress. During that same period, the national savings rate has plummeted from 10 percent to negative territory. It's time to start over with a simple, clear approach.

The purpose of these four incentives is to give every American a simple way to save, invest, and accumulate wealth. Many taxpayers don't use current provisions like the EITC because they're more red tape than they're worth. Trust us: The wealthy never pass up the tax break for capital gains. Ordinary Americans shouldn't have to hire an accountant to get ahead.

Republicans and Taxes

For the past thirty years, the American political debate has been shaped largely by one Republican gambit: scaring ordinary Americans into thinking that Democrats will raise their taxes. The trouble with this notion is that it's simply not true. One of the biggest middle-class tax increases in history—the payroll tax hikes of 1983—was signed into law by Ronald Reagan. It was a Republican, the first George Bush, who said, "Read my lips—no new taxes," then cost himself the presidency by raising taxes in 1990. Bill Clinton raised the top tax rate on the wealthy to 39.6 percent and dramatically expanded the Earned Income Tax Credit, just as he had promised in his campaign to do. The only broad-based tax he increased—which was more than offset by the EITC expansion and later middle-class tax cuts such as doubling the children's tax credit—was a 4.3-cent-a-gallon hike in the gasoline excise tax. (Any time gas prices went up only a nickel, the Bush White House considered it a pretty good week.) The last two Democratic nominees, Al Gore and John Kerry, proposed middle-class tax cuts. In one presidential debate, Kerry turned directly to the camera and said slowly, for all

Americans to hear, "I am not going to raise taxes." Every day, the Bush campaign accused him anyway of trying to raise middle-class taxes.

Teddy Roosevelt wasn't waging class warfare when he supported a progressive tax code at the beginning of the last century. Progressivity isn't a Democratic idea; it's an American one—and Americans would never have gone along with a national income tax without it.

Ironically, the greatest victims of the long-standing GOP tax myth are the very middle-class families the Republicans profess to be championing. In the name of protecting the middle class from imaginary tax increases that Democrats would never even consider, the Bush administration has enacted massive tax cuts for the wealthy that have placed the tax burden more squarely than ever on sagging middle-class shoulders. The *New York Times* estimated that because of the Bush tax cuts, the four hundred taxpayers with the highest incomes now pay income, Medicare, and Social Security taxes amounting to virtually the same percentage of their income as people making $50,000 to $75,000. In 2001, the threat of unfair but politically potent Republican attacks scared many Democratic legislators from red states into mistakenly going along with the Bush tax cuts. They felt they had to vote for tax cuts for the wealthy just to stop Republicans from accusing them of something they would never do: raise taxes on the middle class.

The Ten Percent Solution: A Middle-Class Flat Tax

It's time to show once and for all that Democrats will cut middle-class taxes, not raise them. First, to prove to the middle class that we want their taxes to go down, not up, we're prepared to make them an offer that Republicans have refused. We call it the Ten Percent Solution.

Here's how the idea works: As we've already pointed out, the current tax system is stacked against the ordinary taxpayer. Tax breaks go to those who need them least, while people who play by the rules get the shaft. What irks most Americans about the tax code is not only that it's complex, but that the game is rigged. They're right—just look again at the difference between the wealthiest Americans' tax bracket and the effective tax rate they actually pay. In theory, taxpayers with incomes of $10 million or more are in the 35 percent tax bracket. But according to the *New York Times* survey already mentioned, their average effective rate in 2003—thanks to an average tax cut from Bush of more than $1 million—was 22 percent. In other words, the brackets don't tell the real story: What the wealthy actually pay bears no relation to the higher rates society intended them to pay.

Yet when Democrats set out to restore progressivity and close those loopholes, Republicans blocked any action by pretending that asking the wealthy to pay their share was a tax increase for the middle class. The Ten Percent Solution is designed to bury that myth forever. Under our plan, Democrats and Republicans in Congress would agree to end this phony argument by putting a cap on middle-class taxes. The principle behind this Middle Class Flat Tax is simple and fair: No middle-class family with an income of under $100,000 should ever have to pay an effective income tax rate of more than 10 percent. If the amount they owe after calculating their taxes is more than 10 percent of their income, they won't have to pay a dime above 10 percent. If what they owe is less than 10 percent, they'll pay the lesser amount.

In other words, the Ten Percent Solution is the opposite of the Alternative Minimum Tax. The Alternative Minimum Tax is designed to make sure the wealthiest pay all they should. The Ten Percent Solution makes sure no middle-class family pays more than it should.

If Republicans want to have a bidding war over how low to cap the effective tax rate for the middle class, we're happy to join in. As long as we're cutting taxes for ordinary families, not the wealthy, the only limitation is what the nation can afford. But we doubt that Republicans will join us in this crusade because holding down taxes for the middle class was never their intent. Their goal was just the opposite: to cut every tax the middle class doesn't pay.

Eliminating the Capital Gains Tax on the Middle Class

Second, the twenty-first-century economy demands a tax code that values wealth *and* work. To help ordinary Americans get ahead in a competitive world, we should eliminate the capital gains tax on the middle class and all who aspire to join it.

The Bush tax cuts spent a fortune to increase the wealth of those who already had it. That's crazy. We ought to do just the opposite, and help those who aren't rich get rich. Under our plan, the middle class will be able to invest for the long haul, tax-free.

According to the Center on Budget and Policy Priorities, a progressive think tank, 54 percent of all income from capital gains and dividends goes to millionaires, and 78 percent goes to those with incomes over $200,000. Executives pay half the rate on their stock profits that many middle-class families pay on their wages.

As Theodore Roosevelt said a century ago, "This conflict between the men who possess more than they have earned and the men who have earned more than they possess is the central condition of progress." We want a country where you don't have to be wealthy to build wealth.

To help pay for these reforms, we need to take commonsense steps to close loopholes that don't belong there. The good news is, we can have a tax code that is flatter *and* more progressive. The unkindest cuts in the Bush years were the loopholes. No matter how often Republicans promise a simpler code, they seem more interested in littering it with special favors. Get rid of the loopholes, and the broad middle class will reap the benefits.

The Wyden-Emanuel plan for a corporate flat tax will level the playing field for thousands of businesses that can't afford lobbyists and don't seek out special treatment.

As Professors Joseph Dodge and Jay Soled observed in the journal *Tax Notes,* the U.S. will lose $250 billion in tax revenues over the next decade because of underreported capital gains. Senator Evan Bayh has proposed legislation to close this tax compliance gap by making sure the securities industry reports the same information on capital gains that every employer already provides the IRS on wages.

A lasting economic irony of the Bush years may well be that the administration went so far overboard that its desperate quest to protect narrow interests will backfire and force sweeping, progressive changes in the tax code that are long overdue. Middle-class Americans gave Republicans thirty years, and two big chances, to test their tax cut theory. It's time to give the country what it has always really wanted: a tax code that honors our values and an economic plan that works.

CHAPTER 11

WHO SUNK MY BATTLESHIP?: A New Strategy to Win the War on Terror

We need a muscular, progressive strategy to use all the tools of American power to make America safe in a dangerous world. We cannot win the great struggle against extremism alone; we must enlist our allies in a common mission against the conditions that breed it. We must rebuild and expand our armed forces to confront the new threat. We need a new capacity to counter domestic terrorism. Finally, we need to recognize that wars are won or lost at home—by strengthening American competitiveness, asking all Americans to do their part, and ending our oil dependence so that we control our own destiny.

Five years have passed since America was attacked on 9/11. We've now been fighting the war on terror for longer than it took America to win World War II. Apart from American troops, whose heroism has spanned the generations, our time does not stack up well by comparison. Five years after Pearl Harbor, the U.S. had rallied the world to crush Fascist totalitarianism, launch the United Nations, and rebuild Europe. Five years into the war on terror, the U.S. has splintered the world's resolve to stamp out radical Islamic totalitarianism and weakened those hard-earned historic alliances.

When the Japanese bombed Pearl Harbor sixty-five years ago, FDR understood immediately that everything had changed. So, for that matter, did some of his political opponents. As Charles Peters points out in *Five Days in Philadelphia,* FDR and his most recent Republican opponent, Wendell Willkie, were quick to put the partisan wars behind them in order to win the war that mattered.

But in most respects, remarkably little about American politics changed after 9/11, except for the worse. Republicans tried to brand themselves as the post–9/11 party. The Bush White House sought to give every appearance of being on a permanent wartime footing. The president paid surprise visits to the troops and gave speeches about remaining resolute. The vice president hid in undisclosed secure locations, even when he wasn't hunting. Whenever the economy hit a bump, a domestic problem was ignored, or incompetence in the executive branch escaped scrutiny, the excuse was the same: Not now—we're at war!

Yet long after 9/11, the driving force behind the Bush White House was the same as on 9/10: to seize and exploit every possible partisan advantage. From the president's agenda to the Republican Party's priorities, precious little changed. Every issue, every bill, and every speech followed the same pre–9/11 mantra: Put politics first.

If the White House had ever looked beyond the political cycle, the president could have used 9/11 to give Americans the clearest sense of purpose they've had since World War II. For a brief, shining moment, Americans were more united than ever before, and the world was united in sympathy with our cause. Yet within months, President Bush fractured a historic alliance around the world. And in the 2002 and 2004 elections, he resumed the empty, divisive politics that had left us adrift in the first place. Both times, the GOP shamelessly waved the bloody shirt.

Most presidents would have welcomed the kind of bipartisan support that Democrats gave Bush in the wake of 9/11. But in 2002, President Bush went so far as to manufacture a difference so that his party could reap all the political advantage. First, he embraced Democrats' proposal to create a Department of Homeland Security; then he created a phony battle over civil service rules to try to make it look as if Democrats were against an idea he had stolen from them. To rub salt in the wound, Republicans demagogued the issue in vicious campaign ads questioning the security credentials of then Senator Max Cleland, who lost three limbs fighting for his country in Vietnam. In 2004, Bush supporters ran the same ugly play again with Swift Boat ads against John Kerry, another decorated

Vietnam hero. If Karl Rove could have had his way, Bush's reelection slogan would have been "Four More Wars!"

Bush and Rove didn't execute this cynical strategy because 9/11 and the terrorist threat had somehow transformed their worldview. The fact that they tried to squeeze every drop of political juice out of 9/11 is proof that it hadn't changed their worldview much at all. In past wars, Republican and Democratic presidents alike sought the broadest possible support, without regard to party. This president pursued an unprecedented domestic political strategy of divide and conquer. If any Democrats were still living in a pre–9/11 world, they were not alone—the Bush administration got there first.

In both parties, some were slow to grasp the full consequence of 9/11. Frustrated by the absence of progress on the economy and health care, some Democrats couldn't wait to return to the domestic agenda. Understandably, Democrats could not resist protesting a scheming, secretive, politically obsessed White House bungling a costly war—even though angry protesters were exactly the opponent this scheming, secretive, politically obsessed White House wanted.

Rove invented a perpetual-motion machine: Republicans fail on national security, which invites Democratic criticism, which lets Republicans attack Democrats for lack of resolve, which buys Republicans more time to fail on national security.

Beyond the War Room

Like all Americans, we're overwhelmed with gratitude to and admiration of the soldiers and reservists who have risked everything for their country. We pray democracy will take root in Iraq. We're thrilled that Saddam Hussein is rotting behind bars. But we fear that Washington will fail to learn the right lessons from mistakes in Iraq just as the Bush administration learned the wrong ones from 9/11.

While Republicans' leading foreign policy strategists were hopelessly mired in recriminations, many of the best Democratic thinkers began to outline a refreshingly hard-nosed and intelligent new approach. *With All Our Might,* an anthology edited by Will Marshall of the Progressive Policy Institute, spells out a doctrine of "progressive internationalism," which breathes new life into the Democratic vision of Franklin Roosevelt, Harry Truman, and John Kennedy: support for military strength, alliances, and liberal democracy in the world, along with national unity, service, and economic strength at home. In his recent book, *The Good Fight,* Peter Beinart explains why a tough new national security policy is as essential to the future of progressive politics as a united front against totalitarianism and communism was to the New Deal and the Great Society.

As these authors make clear, winning at war is not a partisan or ideological question, as many on the right and some on the left believe, but a fiercely pragmatic one. We won't win the war on terror if both parties are preoccupied with doing battle among themselves and with each other. We won't win it by doubting one another's patriotism or resolve. The American people don't care which party wins, just that America wins.

It is time to close down the political "war rooms" and figure out how to win the war.

The Allies

If we leave the finger-pointing behind (tempting as it may sometimes be) and check our politics at the door, the task at hand becomes clearer, if still daunting. First, we must stop trying to win this struggle on our own. We must be willing to use force, as necessary, to win the war on terror. But military might is just one weapon in our arsenal; American political, moral, and economic leadership is every bit as vital. That means reforming and strengthening multilateral institutions for the twenty-first century, not walking away from them. By pulling out of important international agreements like the Kyoto protocol, the Bush administration hurt America's cause on other fronts.

We should revitalize these strategic alliances. For example, Anne-Marie Slaughter, dean of the Woodrow Wilson School at Princeton, has proposed a new division of labor in which the United Nations takes on economic and social assistance and an expanded NATO takes over the burden of collective security. Reforming the United Nations is hard work; so is bringing the world to a climate change agreement. But walking away from these issues only makes our job even harder. From Iran to North Korea to the Arab street, America can't stop the emergence of new nuclear states, contain loose nukes, or disrupt Al Qaeda all on its own.

THE TROOPS

Second, if we are to win the war that we have, we must rebuild the army we need. Our friend Paul Begala's motto has become "It Takes a Battalion"—and he's right. We cannot fight and win a long war without more troops. When George Bush ran for president in 2000, he complained that the military had been hollowed out. That wasn't true then, but it is true now. Under Donald Rumsfeld, the Pentagon engaged in a drawn-out debate about military transformation but gave short shrift to the basic needs of the soldiers, the heart and soul of our military might. The army doesn't have enough troops, the National Guard and the Reserves are exhausted to the breaking point, and the soldiers we send into battle don't always get the equipment they need to survive.

A 2006 study sponsored by the Pentagon complained that the Army has become "the thin green line." Iraq stretched our forces so thin that soldiers, members of the Guard, and Reservists carried a load far beyond what they had signed up for. The administration jeopardized the success of our mission in Afghanistan by shifting troops to Iraq because it didn't have enough to go all out in both places. Osama bin Laden got away at Tora Bora in part because we didn't have the personnel to pursue him.

We're all for smart weapons, cutting-edge technologies, and even research into missile defense. But if we're serious about winning a long war, we must put first things first: We need a bigger, better-equipped army. And we need to recognize military service as the highest calling a nation can ask.

Today, about 1.5 million Americans are on active duty in the armed forces—half a million in the Army, around 400,000 in both the Navy and the Air Force, and under 200,000 in the Marines. Twenty years ago, at the height of the Cold War, our total troop strength was more than 2.1 million.

The war on terror poses different threats and requires a much more nimble response. But as we have learned the hard way in Iraq and Afghanistan, there is no substitute for troops.

It is time for the U.S. to close the troop gap. Last year, seven Democrats (Senators Joseph Lieberman, Hillary Rodham Clinton, Bill Nelson, Jack Reed, and Ken Salazar, and Representatives Ellen Tauscher and Mark Udall) introduced the United States Army Relief Act. Based on the work of Third Way, a Washington policy group, the bill would add 100,000 soldiers to the Army, the branch of the armed forces that has shrunk the most since the Cold War. The Pentagon also should increase troop strength to bolster the Special Forces and the Marines, so that the U.S. has the ability to respond swiftly in the multiple potential theaters of this long war.

At the same time, we need to make sure that the Pentagon never again sends soldiers into battle without the equipment to succeed and survive there. When a soldier pressed him on that question at a 2004 town hall meeting with troops in Kuwait, Rumsfeld blithely told the GIs, "As you know, you go to war with the Army you have. They're not the Army you might want or wish to have at a later time." Bush should have fired him on the spot for dereliction of duty: failing his solemn responsibility to give the Army he had the help it had to have.

How can we pay for more troops? We could start by improving the efficiency of the Defense Department's procurement system. According to the Government Accounting Office, the Comanche helicopter is $3.7 billion over budget; the F-22A Raptor tactical fighter jet is $10.2 billion over budget; the F-35 Joint Strike Fighter aircraft is $10.1 billion over budget; and the Space Based Infrared Systems High satellite system is $3.7 billion over budget. That's $28 billion in cost overruns on four weapons systems alone—including $1.7 billion in performance incentives that the Pentagon gave contractors anyway.

A stronger army isn't just about troop counts and body armor. In large part, the strength of an army comes from the support it receives from back home. By that measure, our nation's policies have a long way to go in acknowledging the war we're in and the men and women we depend on to win it.

When our troops come home, they deserve a hero's welcome. We propose a new GI Bill for troops and National Guard members and Reservists who have served six months in Iraq and Afghanistan. We should ensure each soldier five years of basic health coverage from the military's active duty TRICARE program. We should expand the existing Montgomery GI Bill to provide up to $75,000 of help for college. And we should give the men and women who have served us well $5,000 tax free to put a down payment on a house.

The Intelligence

We must not forget that centralized bureaucracy is the terrorist's best friend. Although the 9/11 attacks are often described as the greatest failure of American intelligence since Pearl Harbor, they were less a failure of intelligence than of organization. A Central Intelligence Agency briefing in June 2001 warned, "Bin Ladin Planning High-Profile Attacks." In July, an FBI agent wrote a memo urging his superiors to determine whether followers of Osama bin Laden were training in flight schools here in the U.S. In August, President Bush's daily intelligence briefing declared, "Bin Ladin Determined to Strike in

U.S." Each lead fell victim to bureaucratic failure: communications breakdowns between the CIA and FBI, misunderstandings between agents and lawyers, too many layers between the front lines and the top brass. As the 9-11 Commission concluded, "Domestic agencies did not know what to do, and no one gave them direction." Bureaucracy turned out to be destiny.

Yet even in the wake of 9/11, much of the federal response was to create more bureaucracy, not less. There is no better symbol of what's wrong with Washington's uninspired answer to 9/11 than the Department of Homeland Security. DHS is another example of that old political standby: Don't just stand there; do something that will keep people from noticing that you're just standing there.

Other leaders in other eras might need years to build a mammoth, ossified, unresponsive bureaucracy. Here the Bush administration did it overnight. Already, DHS has emerged as the most inept conglomerate since MCI WorldCom. When Hurricane Katrina struck New Orleans, the department had none of the pre–9/11 excuses: The severity of the threat had been long established and was widely known, and Mother Nature provided days of warning. But even when DHS could see exactly what was coming—a luxury we're not likely to have in the event of another terrorist attack—the bureaucracy still failed. Michael Brown, the hapless head of the Federal Emergency Management Agency, told the president that the levees might fail and told his higher-ups at DHS once the levees had been breached. Like a train wreck in slow motion, the government knew from one end to the other that it was headed off the rails but couldn't or wouldn't avert the impending disaster.

Congress had scarcely finished its investigation into the bureaucratic failures of 9/11 when it had to retrace the very same ground on the failures after Katrina. In three years, the Department of Homeland Security has gone through numerous strategic plans and become expert at the appearance of reorganization. But the basic problem is endemic: The department has 180,000 employees. The London bombings in July 2005 were the work of four men with backpacks. Whose organization chart would you rather have?

The Department of Homeland Security is the single biggest obstacle to its own success. Consolidating bureaucracies in Washington is a 1960s answer to a twenty-first-century world. Terrorists are fighting a guerrilla war; we're lining up in rows, as blind to the new era as British redcoats in the Revolutionary War. Against a decentralized enemy, we ought to be pouring our resources into decentralized solutions.

While the administration consolidated the federal government's domestic security functions, it did precious little to strengthen local law enforcement—the front line of homeland defense. And for all its bureaucratic reshuffling, it ignored one of the biggest bureaucratic problems of all—how to compel the CIA and FBI to share intelligence and be more accountable for results.

We have to tackle the intelligence failure head-on. The Bush administration's clumsy disregard of civil liberties and proper oversight leaves America no choice. Like every other democracy on earth, the United States needs to establish a first-class domestic counterterrorism force. Rather than wait for the FBI or CIA to change ancient bad habits, we can deploy an elite squad custom-built for the job: a new Domestic Defense Division that would resemble Britain's successful domestic counterterrorism agency, MI5. In an article for *Blueprint* magazine, former White House crime policy expert Jose Cerda nicknamed the proposed new force "3D."

The sole mission of 3D would be to prevent and preempt terrorism at home. It should include top security talent from the CIA, the FBI, and the ranks of state and local law enforcement.

The Bush administration caused a firestorm when the National Security Agency secretly monitored phone calls and collected Americans' phone records. But the answer is not to curtail domestic intelligence gathering altogether —it's to make sure domestic counterterrorism is done right. First, 3D's work should be given painstaking oversight by the intelligence committees of Congress and intelligence officials from other agencies. Second, as with Britain's MI5, a special tribunal of distinguished federal judges should be established to monitor its activities to make sure that the civil liberties of innocent bystanders are preserved.

We reject the conventional wisdom that the post–9/11 world forces us to choose between our security and our individual freedoms. That's just a bureaucratic excuse for bad police work. With clear rules, careful oversight, and genuine accountability, we can gather intelligence in a way that targets the enemy and leaves law-abiding Americans alone. We can also help government protect another oft-neglected civil liberty: our safety.

The Home Front

Here at home, we must do more to protect vital hard targets that are in private hands, such as refineries and chemical plants. Illinois Senators Dick Durbin and Barack Obama have introduced legislation to require, whenever possible, that the 111 chemical plants nationwide within the vicinity of a million people use safer chemicals that pose less risk in the event of an attack.

We also should be as tough in cracking down on profiteering in the war on terror as the Truman Commission was in scrutinizing financial transactions during World War II. Most companies are scrupulously honest and have done heroic work to support the war effort. Companies that have done otherwise—such as Halliburton, which Pentagon auditors found to have run up more than $1 billion in questionable costs—should pay a heavy price.

To win his era's war, FDR brought the best minds in American business to Washington as dollar-a-year men. As George Bush discovered, you can't win a war by bringing in $500-an-hour lobbyists.

In the end, a nation goes to war, not just a president. Sixty-five years ago, FDR understood that enlisting every American in the war effort was as crucial to defeating Hitler as sending our soldiers off to battle. Once the economy and citizenry of the United States were firing on all cylinders, no nation on earth could stop us. During World War II, most Americans were in less immediate physical danger of enemy attack than we are today, when nerve gas in a subway or a dirty bomb in a backpack can kill thousands at a time. Yet throughout that war, all Americans knew what they had to do—and what they had to do without—for us to win.

In the immediate aftermath of 9/11, Americans were ready and eager to do their part once again. They gave blood, donated millions to help rebuild Lower Manhattan, flew flags from their porches, and lit candles and said prayers for families of the victims. They yearned to do much, much more, but never got the call.

What especially saddens us about the Bush administration's political gamesmanship since 9/11 is that it turned a war that should be every American's fight into just another polarized political issue. Rather than making the war on terror a common cause and part of our daily lives, the administration turned it into another partisan battle for us to watch on cable.

Instead of welcoming the 9-11 Commission as a bipartisan response to tragedy, the Bush White House stalled and stonewalled the commission and failed to enact many of its most important recommendations. Instead of moving aggressively to secure America's borders, Republicans let illegal immigration get out of hand, then tried to take partisan advantage of the backlash. Instead of subjecting domestic intelligence gathering to proper oversight, the Bush administration used its own mistakes as another excuse to attack Democrats as soft on terror.

Bush was justifiably mocked for standing in a flight suit on the USS *Lincoln* in 2003 in front of the banner "Mission Accomplished," but the irony is that he was never able to honestly say, "Mission Defined."

In 2005, the White House hired Professor Peter Feaver, a Duke University expert on wartime communications. He conducted a study of previous wars and concluded that the best way to maintain public support for a war was to tell the American people that it was winning. Under his guidance, the White House published a glossy document on America's plan for victory, which the U.S. generals in Iraq saw only after its release. Americans are born optimists. But in war, the power of positive thinking is not enough. The real key to winning is to carry out a winning strategy—and the key to earning public support for the war on terror is to give every American a role in winning it.

Not only must we ask every young American to serve, but we must challenge every American to do his or her part. Apart from former Department of Homeland Security Secretary Tom Ridge's duct-tape-and-plastic-sheeting fiasco, the government has neither told people what to prepare for nor required them to be prepared. If we're at war and in danger, the national government has a moral duty to tell people exactly what to do about it. The government's job is to do everything in its power to keep citizens safe. Citizens' job is to do everything in their power to help.

Ultimately, the war on terror is a battle for the hearts and minds of humankind. In that battle, the power of our example is America's greatest ally. Even as we fortify our military leadership, we must also strengthen our moral leadership—our sense of responsibility, our ideals and freedoms, our community and diversity, our belief in education and opportunity for all. The best way to stop terrorists from spreading hatred is for us to be a beacon of opportunity and freedom that leads people all over the world to embrace our ideals for themselves.

Our soldiers shouldn't be the first and only ones to sacrifice. All of us have a responsibility to make our country stronger. Young people can do their part through universal citizen service. Successful businesses and individuals can do their part by demanding a smart economic strategy for the nation, not special favors for themselves. Washington can do its part by putting long-term national interests ahead of narrow political ones.

And if we want to show the world that 9/11 made us stronger and smarter, we must also lead the way in building an economy that doesn't run on gasoline.

CHAPTER 12

MEET THE JETSONS: The Hybrid Economy

From the railroad to the automobile to the moon mission, America has always been where the future is made. Today, we have the chance—and the obligation—to do it again, by seizing the frontier of energy-efficient technology, which has the potential to transform our economy as much in the next decade as the Internet did in the last. Energy is a rare public policy issue that can offer a hat trick: creating new jobs, saving the planet, and reducing dependence on a region that has put our security at risk.

For most Americans, 9/11 crystallized these issues in a way that even the OPEC spikes of the 1970s and the Iran hostage crisis did not. As author and columnist Thomas Friedman has repeatedly stressed, we now see that we're not just paying a fortune for oil but paying it to backward regimes that are responsible for the emergence of a terrorist jihad against us.

If, in the midst of the war on terror, the *New York Times* uncovered a secret plot to divert nearly $50 billion a year to the other side, brickbats would fly from one end of Pennsylvania Avenue to the other. But for all the Republicans' chest beating about terrorism, their response to America's oil-for-terrorism scandal has been to look the other way. No issue illustrates better than energy how little 9/11 changed politics as usual in Washington.

Early in 2006, with the price of gasoline and home heating oil soaring, President Bush finally mentioned that the U.S. is "addicted to oil." But his administration and this Congress never even showed up at the methadone clinic. The last energy bill contained $14.6 billion in giveaways to the industry. We will never end our addiction to oil until we overcome our addiction to old politics. We need a comprehensive, forward-thinking energy policy based on efficiency and innovation.

Cutting Gasoline Consumption in Half

First, we should break our oil habit and save our auto industry in the bargain by ushering in a Hybrid Economy that can cut America's gasoline consumption in half over the next decade. Detroit is on the ropes for a host of reasons, from high health care costs to corporate bad judgment. But the biggest looming threat to its survival may be Japan's massive lead in developing hybrid-powered engines. Toyota plans to sell a million hybrids a year by early in the next decade. Ford didn't even introduce a hybrid vehicle until 2005, years after the Toyota Prius and the Honda Insight. GM is still developing its first fully hybrid vehicle. This isn't the first time Japan has taught Detroit a lesson. In the early 1980s, U.S. automakers were in dire straits for the same reason: While Ford and GM were still peddling gas-guzzling Lincolns and Buicks, fuel-efficient Hondas and Toyotas stole a big share of the American market from under their noses.

When we were kids, we used to watch the Shell gasoline ads of drivers on the Bonneville Salt Flats, trying to prove that the company's "extra mileage ingredient," Platformate, would squeeze out a few extra yards per gallon. Today, we have the chance to achieve a real breakthrough: the plug-in hybrid. Hybrid engines save gasoline by switching back and forth from battery to gasoline power. Plug-in hybrids have the potential to store up enough battery power to run an engine for twenty miles without using a drop of gasoline. This isn't some distant dream; we have the technology today. With a plug-in hybrid, commuters can drive back and forth to work, recharge their cars overnight, and go a month or more without a trip to the gas station. Because the electrical grid has surplus capacity at night, when most Americans are asleep, we could recharge millions of plug-in engines during off-peak hours with the existing power plants. A plug-in hybrid engine that runs on a combination of battery power and cellulosic ethanol made from plant waste could get between one hundred and three hundred miles per gallon of gasoline.

At the same time, we should put the tax code in line with the hybrid revolution. Instead of providing tax breaks for Hummers, as this administration did, we should offer a temporary $7,000 tax credit for purchasing hybrids and other "lean burn" powered vehicles assembled in America. Hybrids have proven wildly successful, but a hybrid-powered vehicle can cost up to $6,000 more than a standard gasoline-powered vehicle. Increasing the credit would remove the cost differential, encouraging consumers to buy more hybrids—and increasing the market demand for auto manufacturers to produce them.

Instead of subsidizing a twentieth-century approach to energy, we should accelerate research into the low-to-zero-emission engines and energy-efficient technology that will dominate the future. Government can use its own purchasing power to set an example. As Senator Hillary Clinton has proposed, the federal government should replace its entire fleet—from the army to the General Services Administration—with fuel-efficient cars and trucks.

Finally, we should launch a truly aggressive campaign to develop new energy technologies. Backing away from the Kyoto agreement on climate change was not only a foreign policy blunder, but an economic one. A climate change agreement would force the U.S. to adopt a real energy plan, and to seize the lead in the development of energy-efficient technologies. Energy efficiency can enable our economy to keep growing, even as we begin to curb our contribution to climate change. For example, the average efficiency of America's ten thousand electric power plants—33 percent—hasn't improved since 1960. Transmission losses on power lines have doubled since 1970. Distributed energy systems like solar and wind power have the potential to achieve efficiencies as high as 90 percent.

Representative Jay Inslee's New Apollo Energy Act, based in concept on President Kennedy's Apollo program to reach the moon, offers a comprehensive solution to our energy crisis by establishing new research programs for clean energy, energy efficiency, fusion technology, and ultradeepwater drilling. It also contains initiatives to reduce greenhouse gases and improve research into climate change. Investing in this Apollo project could yield enough energy to replace within two decades the oil we currently import from the Middle East.

In the same vein, Senator Clinton and Representative Bart Gordon have proposed an advanced research projects agency for energy. Modeled on the defense research effort formed after *Sputnik,* this initiative would sponsor energy research in areas where the risk is high, but so is the potential payoff.

Innovation and Jobs

Besides creating millions of jobs, a new national focus on energy can spur a long overdue return to public investment in the frontiers of scientific research. Throughout our history, the national government has stepped forward to make long-term investments that the nation's economy needed but the private sector could not afford. In the mid-nineteenth century, government helped the railroads secure the land to connect one coast to the other. In the 1950s, the Eisenhower administration did wonders for the nation's productivity by creating the interstate highway system. In the 1970s and 1980s, publicly funded research led to the creation of the Internet, which brought one of the greatest returns on investment in history: a productivity boom that created new industries, transformed old ones, and ushered in a new economic era.

In some respects, we're now living on the fumes of a spectacular era of public research and investment, from NASA's mission to put a man on the moon to the Cold War defense buildup. Publicly funded research is still paying dividends at the National Laboratories, universities, and the National Institutes of Health. But in part because of the success of our past breakthroughs, we need to be investing much more in order to remain at the forefront. Technological breakthroughs now have a shelf life of a few years or less. Meanwhile, competitor nations are pouring resources into research to seize the technological lead.

No country will be able to hold its own in the twenty-first century without a smart national economic strategy. Businesses, not governments, create jobs, but a government that invests in the future can make good jobs more likely. In the 1990s, our administration did everything we could to get Americans ready for the twenty-first century. Unfortunately, the current administration put the ship in reverse. Over the past five years, federal investment in research and development remained flat; in 2005, the president tried to cut funding by $300 million. Budget cuts forced the National Science Foundation to turn down thousands of new research proposals that it otherwise could have funded. The Department of Commerce's Technology Opportunities Program, a federal initiative that promotes an expansion of broadband technology, was zeroed out. Both the president and Congress refused to honor their commitment to double funding for the National Science Foundation. In February 2006, budget cuts forced the layoff of three dozen workers at the National Renewable Energy Laboratory in Colorado. When Bush visited the lab to tout his energy plan a few weeks later, bad publicity forced the administration to scramble to find the money to rehire the workers laid off. If only the future had made it onto Bush's itinerary more often.

With the "future budget" we outlined earlier, we will have an unprecedented opportunity over the next decade to push the frontiers of science and technology in a way that can make our society safer, healthier, and more efficient—and create millions of high-wage jobs. Breakthroughs in energy efficiency, health care, and other areas can help solve problems we desperately need to solve anyway. As we have seen before in the nation's history, the ripple effect of such breakthroughs can put America's middle-class-job machine back in business.

A National Institute of Science and Engineering

Throughout the past century, the United States remained the world's leader in innovation. Yet, in recent years, that role has become increasingly uncertain. Seeking to replicate our success, countries throughout the world have invested in their universities and in research and development. Many countries have begun to reap the benefits of these investments. Each year China produces more engineers than the United States, and European nations have now surpassed the United States in the number of recent scientific research papers published. While our nation faces increased competition from abroad, we have failed in our federal commitment to research and development. Federal funding for research and development as a percentage of GDP fell from 2 percent in the late 1960s to a fifty-year low of 0.7 percent in 2005.

The long-term impact of this neglect is clear. Approximately 50 percent of our economic growth during the past fifty years is attributable to technological innovation. Basic research is the backbone of our innovation economy. Yet, with the exception of the life sciences (like biotechnology and medicine) and defense, funding for research has steadily declined since the 1970s. We spend less on the physical sciences (such as physics and chemistry) than we did fifteen years ago: Their share of the federal research budget has been cut in half since then.

To foster innovation and maintain our advantage in the global marketplace, we should create a National Institute of Science and Engineering. In the past decade, funding for the National Institutes of Health (NIH) has more than doubled and has helped the U.S. remain the world leader in medical technology and medical research. What the NIH has done for medicine, a National Institute of Science and Engineering can do for the physical sciences. This initiative would double the budget of the National Science Foundation, which oversees basic research; venture half the investment for high-risk partnerships with companies and universities; help small businesses bring technological advances to market; and make sure universities, community colleges, and schools have the equipment and expertise to be at the cutting edge of math, science, and engineering.

Increased investment in research will be of little use if we fail to produce enough well-trained young scientists and engineers. According to *Business Week,* the U.S. ranks behind thirteen other countries—including Japan, Germany, and South Korea—in the percentage of its twenty-four-year-olds with a college degree in science and engineering. Twenty-five years ago, we were in third place. The National Science Teachers Association estimates that only a quarter of high school graduates have the skills to complete a freshman science course in college. The results of our lackluster performance are apparent. In 2000, 38 percent of jobs in the United States requiring a Ph.D. in science and technology were filled by people born abroad, up from 24 percent in 1990.

Universal Broadband and High Speed Rail

The national government isn't meeting its responsibility to maintain an economic climate that helps America take the lead. In the 1990s, economic growth exploded in large part because of the national government's support of research into information technology. Such leadership is sorely missing in this decade. Access to broadband, for example, is the password to the new economy. Yet last year, the U.S. fell to twelfth in the world in broadband access. Americans pay twice as much for broadband as the Chinese, and thirty times as much as the Japanese.

The argument for universal broadband—and universal wireless networks—is as strong today as FDR's argument to light the Tennessee Valley in the 1930s. Broadband has the potential to save us billions in health care costs, to reduce energy dependence by allowing more workers to telecommute, and to strengthen our ability to communicate and respond in the event of a terrorist attack. Above all, it can bring the New Economy to rural and neglected parts of America and can help determine whether new jobs land in Bangor or Bangalore. According to a Brookings Institution report, universal broadband could lead to the creation of 1.2 million jobs a year and add $500 billion to the U.S. economy. As Minority Leader Nancy Pelosi has made clear in the House Democrats' Innovation Agenda, the national government is crazy not to do everything in its power—providing tax incentives, supporting technological research, clearing away regulatory hurdles, making more of the spectrum available—to ensure every corner of the country has high-speed access to the global economy.

Another key to a twenty-first-century infrastructure is high-speed rail. Railroads were the engine that drove America's industrial revolution in the nineteenth century. Unfortunately, they haven't changed much since. Today, a rail car takes three days to travel from Los Angeles to Chicago, the nation's transportation hub. Because of outdated, inefficient infrastructure, that same car then takes another three days to travel from the west side of Chicago to the south side.

Railroads are a highly efficient way to move people and goods. It takes only one gallon of diesel fuel to transport a ton of coal four hundred miles by rail. A 25 percent shift of freight from trucks to rail would save fifteen billion gallons a year and save the average commuter forty-two hours a year in traffic. High-speed rail could compete with air travel for trips of up to three hundred miles, saving energy and unclogging our airports and freeways. We ought to make low-interest loans available for high-speed rail projects, and to put the same kind of smart investment into rail transportation that has succeeded with highways and airports.

The real threat of letting the future fend for itself is the great opportunities that will pass us by. In his last speech before he died, JFK said that America was like the country boys who came upon an orchard wall too high for them to climb and threw their caps over the wall so they would *have* to climb it. It is time to toss our caps again, and start climbing.

EPILOGUE

A POLITICS OF NATIONAL PURPOSE

We've tried to offer some new ideas in this book, and we hope they'll inspire others to offer more. But the truth is, none of our new ideas will turn this country around unless America decides to bring back an old idea: responsibility.

Citizenship is not an entitlement program. The precious freedom we enjoy is not free; to preserve and strengthen it, all of us must do our part. As the Declaration of Independence makes clear, we are endowed by our Creator with inalienable rights—and inescapable responsibilities. If we want America to be the land of opportunity, it must be a land of responsibility as well.

We've seen how much weaker we are when we try to live in an era without responsibility. No one will ever forget the shocking image of thousands of poor people in the Superdome after Hurricane Katrina, trapped by neglect even more than by the weather. Corporate shams at Enron and elsewhere rattled our faith in free enterprise. If Americans had any faith in politics, the parade of scandals led by Jack Abramoff shook that, too.

Responsibility begins at the top. That means living up to the highest standards of public service. It means putting the nation's books in balance, not running the country into debt. Above all, it means doing right by the future by making honest, good-faith efforts to solve the country's problems.

But our leaders also have a broader obligation: to make it easier for people to take responsibility in their own lives, and to challenge and inspire them to do so for themselves, their communities, and their country. That's what a social contract is all about: not giving people a program for every problem, but establishing the tools and conditions that will enable them to make the most of their own lives.

Our best leaders have always understood this. The Founders set out "to form a more perfect Union." Abraham Lincoln appealed to "the better angels of our nature." FDR rose from his wheelchair to show Americans how to look past their own pain, and to see how the fight would make us stronger in the end.

In a real Responsibility Era, the poverty we saw on those New Orleans rooftops will not be overlooked or forgotten. In the 1990s, America helped seven million Americans lift themselves out of poverty because we put our government back in line with our values. By expanding the Earned Income Tax Credit, we made work pay better than welfare.

By giving millions of parents the chance to get health coverage for their children, and holding absent parents accountable for child support, we honored family. By spending more on child care and reforming welfare to require work, we gave people a chance to get ahead by putting them to work instead of writing them off by writing them checks for life.

When Bill Clinton ended welfare as we had known it, America responded in heroic ways. Businesses stepped forward to hire and train people. States overhauled their bureaucracies to help recipients find jobs. Most of all, people who had been trapped on welfare flocked to work in record numbers. Child poverty declined by 25 percent, child support collections doubled, and the teen birth rate fell to its lowest level in sixty years.

A decade later, we still have far more work to do to bring everyone into the mainstream of American life. Although single mothers made great strides in the 1990s, low-income men lost ground in the midst of the longest, broadest economic boom in American history. In many neighborhoods today, the culture of fatherhood is as deeply broken as the old welfare system that was so recently fixed. In the same way that we asked more from mothers on welfare, we must now ask low-income fathers to do their part and give them the chance to do so. As Al Gore once proposed, we should dramatically expand drug testing and treatment so that ex-offenders leave jail clean and ready to work. We need to pick up where Clinton left off in steering capital to the inner city, and getting companies to recognize poor urban and rural areas as emerging new markets. We should stop making women carry the whole burden of welfare reform and insist that absent fathers work off the child support they owe.

In a real Responsibility Era, our leaders will unite the nation in an effort to change the culture instead of just leading laments about its decline. We ought to be able to preserve a woman's right to choose and meet Representative Tim Ryan's goal of reducing the number of abortions by 90 percent over the next decade. That means embracing measures that unite Americans in agreement, from teaching pregnancy prevention to promoting adoption to providing health care for pregnant women.

As fathers of young children, we share the anxieties most American parents feel about an intrusive culture pressuring our kids to grow up too fast. Like most parents, we struggle to stand vigil against the ever-changing technologies of cultural attack, and we shudder at the disturbing, parent-free worlds we find at social networking sites that millions of students frequent on the Internet.

Parents should not have to fight this fight alone. We should regulate marketing aimed at children and make sure those in the entertainment industry understand that although the First Amendment is sacrosanct, they have a special responsibility to enrich the culture, not make it more corrosive, and to make art worthy of their talent and worth their own children watching.

In a real Responsibility Era, we will find the sense of community we're all looking for in our sense of common purpose. Washington has forgotten that we're a nation of barn raisers, not fund-raisers, and of shared sacrifice, not special privilege. Americans long for common cause and search for it from book groups in Bethesda to megachurches in Maricopa County. Give everyone a stake in the country's policies, and there's no limit to what we can achieve.

In our time at the White House, the most surprising issue we ever worked on was one of the humblest: school uniforms. In her book, *It Takes a Village,* First Lady Hillary Clinton had praised Long Beach, California, for cutting school violence in half by being the first school district in America to mandate uniforms for elementary and secondary students. When President Clinton challenged communities to adopt school uniforms in his 1996 State of the Union Address, pundits in Washington sneered that they'd never heard such a small idea. But in kitchens and living rooms across the country, parents gushed with exactly the opposite reaction: At last, Washington was addressing an issue that might actually make a difference in their daily lives. By the end of Clinton's presidency, one out of every eight public schools required school uniforms—quadruple the number when he issued the challenge—and school violence went down. Washington called it a small idea; America made it a big success.

As Jonathan Alter of *Newsweek* wrote at the time, Americans understood what many politicians did not: Any idea that succeeds in solving a problem is bigger and more important to people than endless partisan debates in Washington that wind up solving nothing. Unlike politicians, families have to deal with real issues, not phony ones. They know that unless they do something about a problem, it won't go away. That's the fundamental disconnect between the people and their government. These days, politics is all about arguments when it ought to be about finding solutions.

Most of the time, it's the arguments that divide us, not the answers. Even on the most intractable problems, most Americans can find common ground. From reforming welfare to fighting crime to standing up for family values, we've always found that regardless of party, most Americans' true ideology is to do something about it.

Today, most of what we argue about in Washington isn't even the real reason we're arguing. To be sure, we have significant differences on important issues. But the real reason we're at each other's throats is that the problems we ought to be solving are so hard. We haven't faced them long enough to sort out where we might agree—so we try not to face them at all.

The Bush administration carried this kind of politics to

its logical conclusion. At every turn, George Bush tried to make reality fit his ideology. To no avail: From Iraq to Katrina to the deficit, he saw his ideology mugged by reality. Yet a dose of reality is exactly the medicine our ailing political system needs. The clearer the competitive threat from China and India, the more likely we are to rouse ourselves to respond—and when we do, we have the chance to build a stronger, more equitable society than if we had not been so challenged. The more we focus on the hard realities of the war on terror, the more we will do to build a world that looks up to America with respect and wants to emulate our way of life, not destroy it. The more seriously we take the real threats to our culture, the harder we will work to raise our children right, and the prouder we will be of what they become.

In recent years, the red and blue electoral map has led some to conclude that America is hopelessly divided. But like so much in politics, that is an optical illusion. Politics has divided us, but we will not stay divided. Politics has failed us, but as Franklin Roosevelt said, “Failure is not an American habit,” and we will not fail.

For more than two hundred years, this has been the American story: discovering again and again that no challenge is impossible for a nation that rolls up its sleeves and gets to work. The new conditions we must face in this century are daunting. The new arrangements we must make will not be easy or quick. The new certainties we must secure may not fill every void of the old certainties we miss. But if we have the courage, these challenges will give us what America needs most: a mission. There is nothing wrong with our politics or our country that a sense of higher purpose will not fix. We have the will—and we have The Plan. In the strength of great hope, we will once again shoulder our common load.

NOTES

Prologue: Lost and Found

Franklin Roosevelt addressed the Commonwealth Club in San Francisco on September 23, 1932. See the "Top 100 Speeches" at www.americanrhetoric.com. For more on Roosevelt, read Jonathan Alter's *The Defining Moment: FDR's Hundred Days and the Triumph of Hope* (Simon & Schuster, 2006).

Hacks and Wonks

Portions of this chapter first appeared in the March 2004 issue of *Washington Monthly*. Ron Suskind wrote about John DiIulio in the January 2003 issue of *Esquire*. His book is *The Price of Loyalty: George W. Bush, the White House, and the Education of Paul O'Neill* (Simon & Schuster, 2004). Many of O'Neill's own documents from the Bush administration are available at www.ronsuskind.com. Two excellent books on the futility of politics without purpose are E. J. Dionne's *Why Americans Hate Politics* (Simon & Schuster,

1991) and Joe Klein's *Politics Lost: How American Democracy Was Trivialized By People Who Think You're Stupid* (Doubleday, 2006).

The Frame Game

"The Has-Been" has made some of these arguments in *Slate.* George Lakoff's book is *Don't Think of an Elephant! Know Your Values and Frame the Debate* (Chelsea Green, 2004). Thomas Frank's book is *What's the Matter with Kansas? How Conservatives Won the Heart of America* (Metropolitan Books, 2004). For a brief history of how Bill Clinton transformed the Democratic Party, see Al From's November 2005 speech at Hofstra University, entitled "The New Democrat from Hope." One of the best accounts of the 1996 welfare reform law is Jason DeParle's *American Dream: Three Women, Ten Kids, and a Nation's Drive to End Welfare* (Viking Adult, 2004).

Ozzie and Harriet Don't Live Here Anymore

For more on what to do about the collapse of the old economic arrangements, read Gene Sperling's *The Pro-Growth Progressive: An Economic Strategy for Shared Prosperity* (Simon & Schuster, 2005), as well as Thomas L. Friedman's *The World Is Flat: A Brief History of the Twenty-First Century* (Farrar, Straus & Giroux, 2005). See "America Can Do Better," *Blueprint,* November/December 2005; "The Politics of

Opportunity," a May 2006 white paper by Anne Kim and Jim Kessler for Third Way; and "Raising Our Game," by Edward Gresser, *Blueprint*, May/June 2006.

What's the Plan?

Theodore Roosevelt outlined "The New Nationalism" in Osawatomie, Kansas, on August 31, 1910. The phrase comes from the 1909 classic *The Promise of American Life*, by Herbert Croly, who went on to found the *New Republic*.

Asked Not: Universal Citizen Service

We wrote this chapter in memory of our beloved friend, the late Eli Segal, who dedicated his life to service, and who joined with President Clinton to launch the AmeriCorps program and later the Welfare to Work Partnership. See *A History of National Service in America*, edited by Peter Shapiro (Center for Political Leadership and Participation, 1994).

Toga Party: Universal College Access

We consulted persuasive studies by, among others, Michael Dannenberg, Richard D. Kahlenberg, Anthony P. Carnevale, Stephen J. Rose, Thomas G. Mortenson, Paul Weinstein, Jr., and Robert Shireman. For more information on the college opportunity gap, read "A Matter of

Degrees: Improving Graduation Rates in Four-Year Colleges and Universities," by Kevin Carey (Education Trust, May 2004). See also "Cost Remains a Key Obstacle to College Access," by Richard D. Kahlenberg, *Chronicle of Higher Education,* March 10, 2006. Other invaluable sources of information on education policy in the twenty-first century include Achieve (www.achieve.org), Education Sector (www.educationsector.org), and www.solutionsforourfuture.org.

WHO WANTS TO BE A MILLIONAIRE?: UNIVERSAL RETIREMENT SAVINGS

William Gale, Peter Orszag, and Jon Gruber make the case for automatic 401(k)'s in "Improving Opportunities and Incentives for Saving by Middle- and Low-Income Households," an April 2006 white paper from the Hamilton Project of the Brookings Institution. Other leading thinkers who have written about wealth creation include Mark Iwry, Gene Sperling, Rob Shapiro, Adam Solomon, and Paul Weinstein, Jr. The Retirement Security Project is supported by the Pew Charitable Trusts in partnership with Georgetown University's Public Policy Institute and the Brookings Institution. See also "The State of Private Pensions: Current 5500 Data," by Marric Buessing and Mauricio Soto, Center for Retirement Research at Boston College, February 2006.

House Call: Universal Children's Health Care

As we have done for the past fifteen years, we relied on the wisdom of longtime health expert Chris Jennings. For more on health care, see two articles by Ezekiel J. Emanuel and Victor R. Fuchs: "Health Care Vouchers—A Proposal for Universal Coverage," in the March 24, 2005, issue of *New England Journal of Medicine,* and "Getting Covered," in the November/December 2005 issue of *Boston Review.* See also "America's Fragmented Health Care System: The Spiraling Costs We See and the Hidden Costs We Don't," by Laurie Rubiner and Cindy Zeldin, a July 2004 report from the New America Foundation; "A Health Care Promise We Can Keep," by Sarah Bianchi, in the July/August 2003 issue of *Blueprint;* "Fixing America's Health Care System," by David Kendall, a September 2005 report for the Progressive Policy Institute; and the extensive work of the Kaiser Family Foundation. A National Cure Center is the long-standing passion of Lou Weisbach and Rick Boxer.

The Era of Hack Government Is Over: Fiscal Responsibility and An End to Corporate Welfare

See Felix Rohatyn's article, "A Trust Fund for America," in the *Wall Street Journal,* June 16, 2005. Rob Shapiro outlined the concept of a future budget in "Paying for Progress: A Progressive Strategy for Fiscal Discipline," a February 1991 paper for the Progressive Policy Institute. He later wrote a series of papers on the strategy of "cut and invest." Ed Kilgore wrote about redistricting in "The Fix Is In," *Blueprint,* May/June 2005. Portions of this chapter appeared in that same issue in the cover story, "Drain the Swamp!" See "The Road to Riches Is Called K Street," *Washington Post,* June 22, 2005. Jacob Weisberg coined the phrase "interest-group conservatism" in a May 4, 2005, column in *Slate.*

The Ides of April: Tax Reform to Help Those Who Aren't Wealthy to Build Wealth

The opening quote is from Ron Suskind's *The Price of Loyalty.* The *New York Times* analysis of the Bush tax cuts appeared on April 5, 2006. The most devastating criticism of Bush's war on work is still Warren Buffett's op-ed, "Dividend Voodoo," in the May 19, 2003, issue of the *Washington Post.* See also "The Democrats Can Win on Taxes," the *Wall Street Journal,* October 15, 2003; "Family-Friendly Tax Reform," Paul Weinstein, Jr.'s April 2005 report for the Progressive Policy Institute; and "Inflated Tax Basis and the Quarter-Trillion Dollar Revenue Question," by Joseph M. Dodge and Jay A. Soled, *Tax Notes,* January 24, 2005. Much to Republicans' dismay, our tax reform plan will cut taxes for the middle class and those who aspire to join it. For example, a family of three with an $80,000 income and $12,000 in tuition for training currently receives an $850 child credit and a $500 deduction for higher-education expenses. Under our plan, the family would receive a $2,500 Simplified Family Credit and $3,000 from the Refundable Credit for Higher Education Expenses—for a total net tax cut of $4,150 below what they pay now.

Who Sunk My Battleship?: A New Strategy to Win the War on Terror

Will Marshall's outstanding anthology is *With All Our Might: A Progressive Strategy for Defeating Jihadism and Defending Liberty* (Rowman & Littlefield, 2006). Peter Beinart's fascinating book is *The Good Fight: Why Liberals—and Only Liberals—Can Win the War on Terror and Make America Great Again* (HarperCollins, 2006). See also Charles Peters, *Five Days in Philadelphia: The Amazing 'We Want Willkie' Convention of 1940 and How It Freed FDR to Save the Western World* (PublicAffairs, 2005). The 2005 report on "The Thin Green Line" was written for the Pentagon by Lieutenant Colonel Andrew Krepinevich (retired). Thomas Donnelly of the American Enterprise Institute has written extensively about troop strength. See "Stressed Out," by Steven Nider, *Blueprint*, May/June 2004. Some of the arguments in this chapter first appeared in the July/August 2002 issue of *Blueprint.* See also Jose Cerda III's cover story, "Cop Crunch," in the April/May 2003 issue of the same magazine. To read about a president who, unlike Bush, held his generals and Cabinet accountable for results, see

Team of Rivals: The Political Genius of Abraham Lincoln, by Doris Kearns Goodwin (Simon & Schuster, 2005).

Meet the Jetsons: The Hybrid Economy

Al Gore spells out the threat of climate change in *An Inconvenient Truth* (Rodale, 2006), which is now also a powerful documentary film. Jan Mazurek offers a strategy to cap and trade greenhouse gas emissions in "A New Clean Air Strategy," a December 2005 report for the Progressive Policy Institute. More information on plug-in hybrids is available from the California Cars Initiative at www.calcars.org. The House Democrats' Innovation Agenda can be found at www.HouseDemocrats.gov.

Epilogue: A Politics of National Purpose

For more on fatherhood, see the January/February 2002 issue of *Blueprint.* For more on parents, children, and culture, see "Childhood for Sale," an August 2005 report by Michele Stockwell for the Progressive Policy Institute.

ACKNOWLEDGMENTS

Politics is a team sport. Throughout the past twenty years, we have been blessed with the finest of teammates. Everything we know about policy and politics we learned from the elected officials we served, the candidates we campaigned for, the colleagues we worked with, and the voters we worked for.

We are especially grateful to President Bill Clinton, the most successful president in our lifetime, who taught us that opportunity, responsibility, and community could overcome America's toughest challenges. We thank the two leaders who gave us our first jobs in politics, Mayor Richard Daley and former Vice President Al Gore. In particular, Rahm thanks the people of the 5th Congressional District of Illinois, who have taught him firsthand what public service ought to be about.

The Democratic Party is rich with ideas and people who think of them. Many of the best ideas in this book were inspired and shaped by the work of Senator Hillary Clinton's American Dream Initiative for the Democratic Leadership Council, an effort that brought policy thinkers from the Progressive Policy Institute, Third Way, the Center for American Progress, the Hope Street Group, and NDN together with DLC leaders Governor Tom Vilsack, Senator Tom Carper, and other elected officials.

We're grateful to all the public officials whose ideas appear in these pages, and to the many dedicated staffers who work for them. We should single out those who have to put up with Rahm the most—the House Democratic leadership (Representatives Nancy Pelosi and Steny Hoyer), and Illinois's impressive Democratic lineup (including Governor Rod Blagojevich and Senators Dick Durbin and Barack Obama). We extend our gratitude and sympathy as well to all those who work with Bruce at the DLC, especially its founder, Al From, who has spent two decades reminding Democrats how much ideas matter.

We could not have written this book without a great deal of help from all our favorite Wonks, and even a few Hacks. Their names and ideas appear throughout these pages, but the highest tribute we can offer is to point readers to their work, as we have tried to do in the Notes section. Rahm would like to thank the members of his staff, who have worked hard since he was elected on many of the legislative ideas that made it into this book. He is indebted to them for their ingenuity and just plain hard work.

It takes a true friend to read and improve any first draft, and for that, we thank Paul Weinstein, Jr., Chris Jennings, and Gene Sperling. We also thank the great editors—including Peter Beinart, Susan Glasser, Paul Glastris, Steve Mufson, David Plotz, Peter Ross Range, and Jacob Weisberg—who have given us the chance to hone our arguments.

Many others have volunteered wisdom, expertise, support, and friendship: David Axelrod, Paul Begala, Sarah Bianchi, Debbie Boylan, Debbie Cox Bultan, James Carville, Jose Cerda III, Rosa DeLauro, Tom Donilon, Ari Emanuel, Ezekiel Emanuel, Peter and Alison Fenn, Pat and Sue Flammia, Tom Freedman, Sam Fried, Robert Gordon, Stan Greenberg, Christine Hammer, Dena Hirschberg, Susan Hunter, Ed Kilgore, John Kupper, Jim LePard, Tamera Luzzatto, Jerry Mande, Goody Marshall, Will Marshall, Cathy Mays, David Mott, Steven Nider, Holly Page, Mark Penn, Tara Reed, Joe Rimsa, Laurie Rubiner, Ivan Schlager, Bernard Schwartz, Rob Shapiro, Cliff Sloan, Adam Solomon, Tammy Sun, Neera Tanden, Marshall Wittmann, Jerry Woolpy, and Donna and Roger Young.

We are grateful to our legendary agent, Morton Janklow, and to our publisher, PublicAffairs. Our editor, David Patterson, offered the consistently brilliant editorial direction and clarity it took to meet an improbable deadline. Publisher Susan Weinberg also provided superb, pithy editorial advice. Melissa Raymond ably and patiently oversaw production of the book. Margaret Ritchie gracefully copyedited the manuscript. Whitney Peeling proved to be a first-rate publicist on the book's behalf, Nina D'Amario a skilled art director, and Lisa Kaufman and Lindsay Goodman an excellent marketing team. In particular, we thank a man whose vision guided us from start to finish: the extraordinary founder of PublicAffairs, Peter Osnos, who helped change America in the 1990s by publishing *Putting People First*, and who had the wisdom to see that it was time for a change in America again.

Finally, we wish to thank our families. Throughout our careers, our parents have been our inspiration. Ben and Marsha Emanuel have raised three remarkable children and one congressman, and taught them how lucky they were to be Americans. In Idaho, the reddest of states, Scott and Mary Lou Reed have spent half a century fighting for environmental protection, civil rights, and human rights—and they're not done yet.

We wrote this book for our children. Rahm's three favorite constituents didn't even vote for him: Zach, Ilana, and Leah, who suggested we offer America the subtitle, "Roses are red / Violets are blue / This book's about you." In Bruce's eyes, Julia and Nelson will always be the greatest domestic achievements of the Clinton era. They proved to be the best editors a father could want—playing catch with him every day, and just teasing every time they asked if the book was done yet.

For our wonderful children, and for every other happiness in our lives, we thank our amazing wives, Amy Rule and Bonnie LePard. Amy is Rahm's best friend, toughest critic, and true love. Bonnie has been the joy, the spark, the conscience, and the thrill of Bruce's life since high school. The smartest plan Rahm and Bruce ever made was to find life partners who suffer fools gladly and so well.

INDEX

INDEX

INDEX

INDEX

INDEX

PublicAffairs is a publishing house founded in 1997. It is a tribute to the standards, values, and flair of three persons who have served as mentors to countless reporters, writers, editors, and book people of all kinds, including me.

I. F. Stone, proprietor of *I. F. Stone's Weekly,* combined a commitment to the First Amendment with entrepreneurial zeal and reporting skill and became one of the great independent journalists in American history. At the age of eighty, Izzy published *The Trial of Socrates,* which was a national bestseller. He wrote the book after he taught himself ancient Greek.

Benjamin C. Bradlee was for nearly thirty years the charismatic editorial leader of *The Washington Post.* It was Ben who gave the *Post* the range and courage to pursue such historic issues as Watergate. He supported his reporters with a tenacity that made them fearless, and it is no accident that so many became authors of influential, best-selling books.

Robert L. Bernstein, the chief executive of Random House for more than a quarter century, guided one of the nation's premier publishing houses. Bob was personally responsible for many books of political dissent and argument that challenged tyranny around the globe. He is also the founder and was the longtime chair of Human Rights Watch, one of the most respected human rights organizations in the world.

. . .

For fifty years, the banner of Public Affairs Press was carried by its owner Morris B. Schnapper, who published Gandhi, Nasser, Toynbee, Truman, and about 1,500 other authors. In 1983 Schnapper was described by *The Washington Post* as "a redoubtable gadfly." His legacy will endure in the books to come.

Peter Osnos, *Founder and Editor-at-Large*